T0294706

LIONS
IN THE
WILDERNESS
England's Decade of Decline

LIONS
IN THE
WILDERNESS
England's Decade of Decline

Clive Hetherington and Joe Hetherington
FOREWORD BY MALCOLM MACDONALD

First published by Pitch Publishing, 2024

Pitch Publishing
9 Donnington Park,
85 Birdham Road,
Chichester,
West Sussex,
PO20 7AJ
www.pitchpublishing.co.uk
info@pitchpublishing.co.uk

ISBN 978 1 80150 719 6

Typesetting and origination by Pitch Publishing
Printed and bound in India by Replika Press Pvt. Ltd.

Contents

To Linda, Emily, Jane, Luke and Maisie

Acknowledgements

Sincere thanks go to the following for their help and co-operation in the composition of this book:

Malcolm Macdonald, David Mills, Bryan 'Pop' Robson, Terry McDermott and the late Gordon McQueen.

Foreword

I DON'T think it was just the England football team who underachieved in the 1970s – I think it was the whole game in this country.

One of the reasons was that there was such a fear of television. There were hardly any live games on TV in the belief that nobody would turn up at the grounds to see matches. It was thought they would all sit at home and watch them on TV. That proved to be totally off the mark.

I looked at other countries and they seemed to be getting it right at that time – and English football got it wrong. It wasn't until the 1980s that it started to change.

There wasn't the flow of money coming into the game that allowed clubs to really improve themselves as they are able to do now. The game was very much in the doldrums.

When I scored my five goals for England against Cyprus in 1975, the game wasn't live on TV. It was recorded highlights in the evening. The nation was being denied seeing its national team playing live.

England players like Jimmy Greaves and Gerry Hitchens went to play in Italy in the 1960s and Kevin Keegan went to play in West Germany in the 1970s.

But you didn't get Italians or Germans coming to play in England because the game, the whole industry, was backward.

The game was being held back by the people who had control of it. That's why the Premier League came into being in 1992. There were visionaries, some who had never been involved in football before, and they saw what a huge prospect the game was for the world.

A consequence of the English game being behind the times in the 1970s was how we failed at international level. Not only were the players being held back, we didn't have the training facilities like they had throughout Europe. When I signed for Newcastle United in 1971, at our training ground we changed in a cricket pavilion.

Around 1973 or '74, Anderlecht, a top side in Europe at the time, came to an agreement with Newcastle for me. The Belgian FA were hugely advanced compared to the governing bodies in England and the way the transfer operated was, once agreeing a sum, one third of the fee would go to the player. They agreed £300,000, and Newcastle suddenly realised they would only get £200,000 because it was under Belgian FA rules. Of course, the transfer didn't happen and it never went out publicly. The way things were, English clubs pretty much couldn't do any business with European clubs.

We lagged behind in so many ways. In Germany, the top players retired and ended up with top jobs. Franz Beckenbauer won the World Cup as captain of West Germany in 1974 and manager in 1990 – and ended up managing Bayern Munich then becoming their president.

Bobby Moore was England's captain when they won the World Cup in 1966, but after he retired he struggled to get a job in football. He was manager at Southend United but he'd never played at that level. You would have thought he would have had an honorary position, not only at West Ham where he played for so long, but with the FA. Once Sir Alf Ramsey had left him out of the England squad, the FA didn't want to know him. It was quite cruel. They were ignorant of the great names with great experience.

Malcolm Macdonald
Former Newcastle United and England striker

Prologue

All Not Well

ASK A Scot, especially one of a certain vintage, when it was that England were deposed as champions of world football, and they will more than likely say it was 15 April 1967.

It was then that a Jim Baxter-inspired Scotland became the first side to beat England since Sir Alf Ramsey's men had overcome West Germany 4-2 to win the World Cup in 1966. Wembley, the scene of that treasured triumph, also witnessed a tumultuous taming of the Three Lions when the Scots made their then-biennial excursion south of the border. On the occasion in question, the traditional British Home Championship, involving England, Scotland, Northern Ireland and Wales, was doubling up over two seasons as a first-round qualifying group for the European Championship.

England would, ultimately, reach the semi-finals of the tournament in Italy in the summer of 1968, when they lost 1-0 to Yugoslavia in Florence before securing a third-place finish with a 2-0 win over the Soviet Union in Rome. The Scots, meanwhile, had to be content – and certainly were – with a victory they will always cherish. Officially, though, it only brought with it the title of British champions. Maverick Baxter, a Glasgow Rangers icon and at the time playing for Sunderland in the English First Division, was England's tormentor-in-chief, mocking them with an exhibition of ball-juggling dubbed 'keepie uppies'. The Fife-born left-half with the moniker 'Slim Jim' humiliated the hosts who, after going three games unbeaten as World Cup holders, showed a change for the first time to the side that had faced the Germans. Jimmy Greaves suffered anguish when injury curtailed his involvement in 1966 after he had appeared in the opening three World Cup matches, but he was back in attack, replacing Roger Hunt. Greaves, however, was to be one of three walking wounded, along with Jack Charlton and Ray Wilson, in an England side who felt the full force of Scotland's commitment.

The audacious Baxter may have stolen the show with his supreme skills, but it was striker Jim McCalliog who scored what proved to be the decisive goal. Bobby Charlton, in those days the axis of England's team, later confessed that he feared Scotland would be the ones to burst the bubble of their great rivals – because the fixture meant more to them than it did to the English. The defeat, on the sixth anniversary of England's 9-3 Wembley walloping of the Scots, was also the home side's first in 20 matches and it was celebrated by the visiting fans with a pitch invasion that saw the hallowed turf being dug up as a keepsake of a momentous success. The Tartan Army, who would inflict similar destruction on 'the home of football' ten years later, declared Scotland the new world champions.

But, while the Scots have their tongue-in-cheek take on England's demise, it was, of course, a defeat by the same 3-2 scoreline that marked the true end of their time as holders of the Jules Rimet Trophy. That came in the stifling heat of the World Cup in Mexico more than three years later – and England had been warned. In June 1968, West Germany beat the English for the first time, winning 1-0 in a friendly – if there is such a thing when these nations clash – in Hannover with a Franz Beckenbauer goal. When the sides next met, as well as being number one in the world of football, England had also been number one in the UK pop charts with 'Back Home' – a song written by a Scotsman, Bill Martin, and an Irishman, Phil Coulter. It was the World Cup squad's salute to fans the length and breadth of England who would be supporting them from their armchairs while they were, as the lyrics said, far away.

Then came the fateful day. The dateline: 14 June 1970. The venue: León. And following an agonising quarter-final, the message was loud and clear to the folks back home – West Germany had gained revenge for 1966. Most believe that England would have won had it not been for the absence of first-choice goalkeeper Gordon Banks, whose unavailability due to a stomach upset which struck him on the eve of the game was a shock to the system in every respect. Conspiracy theories abounded about whether Banks had somehow been nobbled.

In Jeff Powell's authorised biography *Bobby Moore: The Life and Times of a Sporting Hero*, England captain Moore mused, 'Like the rest of the lads, I was sure Banksie would be all right on the day. Sure enough, he said he felt better next morning. I forgot all about it until we were getting on the coach to drive to the stadium, no more than an hour and a half before the kick-off. Suddenly, Gordon had been taken bad again over lunch. Suddenly, we were on the coach and no Banksie.'

Whatever the whys and wherefores, Peter Bonetti had to deputise and was at least partly at fault as West Germany fought back to turn the match on its head in spectacular fashion. Ramsey felt England had been victims of the vagaries of fate, complaining bitterly after the game that, of all the people to lose, it had to be Banks. But what made the loss, and its consequences, so unpalatable and even harder to come to terms with from the point of view of England fans was the fact that their side had thrown away a two-goal lead and dominated the Germans for much of the match.

The nation was crestfallen and such was the devastating impact on the collective English psyche that some, even to this day, claim it was a contributory factor in Labour prime minister Harold Wilson's surprise defeat by Conservative leader Edward Heath in the general election, which was held only four days later.

So began a decade of decline, a period during which the country was plunged into an economic crisis – and England failed to appear at another major tournament. It would be a turbulent time that would see Ramsey's managerial tenure end in undeserved ignominy and his ultimate successor, Don Revie, incur the wrath of the nation for the unseemly manner in which he left his post.

England's world, however, had in some ways begun to fall apart before a ball was kicked in Mexico. And defensive cornerstone Moore, the face for many of their finest hour in 1966 when he held aloft the World Cup, would find himself centre stage for very different reasons.

1

A World Away

THE 1970 FA Cup Final, one of the most memorable in the rich history of the competition, was an important precursor to the World Cup from an England perspective. The domestic showpiece was brought forward to April from its traditional May date to assist in England's preparations for that summer.

Deadly rivals Chelsea and Leeds United slugged it out in an epic, brutal and bruising battle which required a replay – the first in an FA Cup Final since 1912 – and extra time on both occasions, making for four hours of cramp-inducing action. Sir Alf Ramsey had plenty invested in the struggle as no fewer than six of the squad he took to Mexico – the Leeds quartet of Terry Cooper, Jack Charlton, Norman Hunter and Allan Clarke, plus Chelsea's Peter Bonetti and Peter Osgood – figured in both games, as did United pair Paul Madeley and Mick Jones, and John Hollins of the Blues, who had all either been in the England manager's thoughts or were on the periphery of his plans.

Wembley's normally pristine playing surface had been reduced to near-quicksand, but it was testimony to the skill, fitness and endeavour of the two sides that the national stadium still put on a classic final as Chelsea came from behind twice to force a 2-2 draw after goals by Charlton and Jones had given Leeds a whiff of victory. The replay at Old Trafford, 18 days later, was watched by a television audience of 28 million, only bettered by that which tuned in for the World Cup Final four years earlier, and proved to be an even more physical game than the first. In one of several ugly clashes on the night, Charlton launched himself into Osgood, who was left prostrate next to the touchline, in a furious response to the striker's challenge from behind. That exchange epitomised the enmity between the teams. It also featured two players who were destined to put their differences aside and join forces not too long after this bone-jarring tussle, which took place on the penultimate day of April. Jones scored again for Leeds, but Osgood replied late in the game to take it to the extra half hour, during which defender David Webb netted the winner.

The calendar year for England had begun with two friendlies featuring Nottingham Forest forward Ian Storey-Moore's one appearance in a 0-0 Wembley draw against the Netherlands and Osgood's baptism in a 3-1 win in Belgium – Alan Ball scoring in the 27th minute and on the hour in a frantic three-goal, five-minute phase which started with World Cup Final hat-trick hero Geoff Hurst's effort before Jean Dockx pulled one back in the 58th minute.

Then came the British Home Championship, England drawing 1-1 with Wales at Cardiff City's Ninian Park where, with the exception of Emlyn Hughes at left-back instead of Cooper, Ramsey named the side that would start against Brazil that summer. Against Wales, Francis Lee had to level inside the last 20 minutes after midfielder Dick Krzywicki had scored his first and only goal in his country's colours shortly before half-time. Next, Northern Ireland were beaten 3-1 at Wembley, with Martin Peters heading in Bobby Charlton's right-wing corner after only five minutes. Charlton's Manchester United colleague George Best, however, came up with a familiar stroke of genius, bamboozling Bobby Moore and beating Gordon Banks sublimely at his near post with a precise finish five minutes into the second half. Hurst headed home with the aid of a huge deflection after 56 minutes and Charlton slid in to score from a Hughes centre that keeper Pat Jennings could only help across the face of goal nine minutes from time. Manchester United's Brian Kidd and Burnley's Ralph Coates debuted for England. A dour goalless draw against Scotland followed at Hampden Park, leaving England with a superior record to the rest. But the title at that time was purely decided on points and three sides finished with four, meaning England had to share the championship with Wales and the Scots.

Ramsey headed for the World Cup with a 28-man squad, having also named 12 'reserves'. Leeds right-back Paul Reaney had been in the provisional 28 and expected to make the final group of 22, but was ruled out after suffering a broken leg in a game at West Ham near the end of the season. Ramsey had turned to Reaney's colleague, Madeley, who could play anywhere across the back four but was a surprise omission in the first place from the pool of 40 players. In anticipation of being idle that summer, however, Madeley had already made family arrangements and declined Ramsey's invitation. It was an echo of Everton centre-back Brian Labone's decision to stick with marriage plans in the summer of 1966 rather than be part of what proved to be England's greatest achievement. Many feel he would have lined up in the final against West Germany, instead of Jack Charlton. Labone, though, was certainly on board for Mexico.

Madeley's opt-out meant Arsenal left-back Bob McNab, who was among the reserves, was given the nod to join the squad for warm-up games in Colombia and Ecuador, which were tailored to the need to acclimatise to the conditions at altitude in Mexico. But when Ramsey made his final selection, trimming his party to the requisite 22 following those two matches, McNab was one of the six players discarded. The others were Peter Shilton – many had tipped the Leicester goalkeeper to make the squad – midfielder Coates, striker Kidd and his Manchester United team-mate, utility man David Sadler, plus Liverpool winger Peter Thompson, who had to endure the cruellest cut for a third consecutive World Cup after missing out on Chile in 1962 and in 1966. 'Most unfortunate,' Ramsey said of Thompson's omission, 'but one cannot get sentimental.'

It was fair to say that Ramsey had been spoilt for choice, though the way he arrived at his final squad was strangely haphazard for a manager with a reputation for being fastidious. That said, the squad he took to Mexico is widely regarded as the best in England's history, boasting greater strength in depth than that which he had assembled four years earlier. If mulling over his squad had been Ramsey's preoccupation, on 18 May he suddenly had a more pressing concern that was to prove an enormous distraction and mark the most worrying time of his tenure as England manager. Moore, such a dignified figure at the previous tournament, became embroiled in an embarrassing episode in the build-up to the Mexican fiesta.

England had flown to Bogotá to take on Colombia, but shortly after their arrival, a browsing Moore was accused by a shop assistant, Clara Padilla, of stealing a bracelet worth around £600 from the Fuego Verde (Green Fire) jewellery store at the Hotel Tequendama, where England were staying. Police appeared on the scene and, after questioning Moore and Bobby Charlton, who had visited the shop with him but was not under suspicion, they seemed satisfied there had been no wrongdoing.

Moore maintained his innocence and the matter appeared to have been dropped as he played in England's 4-0 beating of Colombia. Peters scored two characteristic headers in the second and 39th minutes, drifting into space at both posts, before Bobby Charlton rifled in a rising right-footed drive ten minutes into the second half and the outstanding Ball nodded in Cooper's cross in the 84th minute with the assistance of goalkeeper Otoniel Quintana's fumble. The game formed part of a double-header for England, who before the main event at the same venue also fielded a side in an unofficial match against Colombia. It was, to all intents and purposes, a B international, and Jeff Astle scored the only goal of the game. Ramsey was content with what he had seen. He said, 'I was very pleased with both matches. No players complained about the altitude.'

Then came the visit to Ecuador, where England won 2-0. The game in Quito was almost played at walking pace at times in the rarefied atmosphere, but Lee gave England a fifth-minute lead when he latched on to full-back Keith Newton's right-wing ball. Hurst had a half-chance to add to the score, but Banks was called on to rescue his side, denying Patricio Penaherrera in a one-on-one after Ball had gifted possession to the attacker. It was late in the game before England settled the outcome. Kidd, who came off the bench 20 minutes from time to replace Lee, grabbed what was to be the only goal of his international career on his second and final appearance. Within seven minutes of entering the fray, he flung himself to head in at the far post from a right-sided centre by Peters after Hurst had looked to glance the ball on.

Meanwhile, back in Colombia and unbeknown to the England party, the finger of suspicion had lingered in Moore's direction. En route to Mexico, the travel schedule necessitated a return to Bogotá on 25 May. It was then that what became known as the 'Bogotá Bracelet' incident erupted into a major diplomatic row.

On their return to the Hotel Tequendama, where they were to kill time awaiting their connecting flight, Ramsey attempted to keep his players entertained by arranging a showing of a western movie. Moore's treatment by the Colombian authorities had become almost akin to something out of the Wild West. When England arrived back at the airport in Bogotá, he was told he had to report to a police station to complete what was assumed to be the formality of confirming the statement he had made over the alleged theft of the mysterious bracelet. Yet had it not been for the careful diplomacy of the British *charge d'affaires*, Keith Morris, police would have arrested Moore in a conspicuous manner at the airport. As it was, a bemused Moore ended up being detained and placed under house arrest. It was agreed that he would be taken to the residence of the Colombian Football Federation president, Alfonso Senior Quevedo, with police officers assigned to guard the England captain. Even Harold Wilson intervened and faced accusations of trying to win votes ahead of the general election – for all the good it did him given the eventual outcome at the polls.

There were claims that Moore had been framed in a plot to undermine England's World Cup campaign. Indeed, the local chief of police suggested it was an elaborate setup. Any case against Moore fell apart when Padilla's account of what happened was debunked during a showy re-enactment in the jewellery shop. After being held for three days, Moore was finally released – only five days before England were due to begin their defence of the World Cup against Romania in Guadalajara. Ramsey and the rest of the squad had already flown to Mexico and before Moore linked up with them again he had an overnight stop in Mexico City where Jimmy Greaves, a competitor in the World Cup Car Rally, paid his West Ham team-mate a surprise visit to lift his spirits with a drink or two. Moore's international career would already be over when, more than five years later, word came from the Foreign Office that the Colombians had declared the Bogotá case closed. In 2003, just over a decade after his death, it emerged in papers released by the Public Record Office that the British Embassy had been informed in the weeks following the allegations against Moore that police in Bogotá had identified the suspected culprit, who had no links whatsoever with the England party.

* * *

Ramsey welcomed Moore back into the fold when he arrived in Guadalajara and any fears about his fitness and preparedness to lead England into the game with Romania were soon allayed. England began the group stage with a 1-0 win, courtesy of Hurst's composed, close-range finish in the 65th minute, when he neatly gave his man the slip at the back post and fired in following Ball's right-flank cross and Lee's flick-on. It was a less-than-convincing victory, but one achieved in the face of provocation from physical opponents. Romania's arch hatchet man was Mihai Mocanu, whose brutish tackling forced off Newton and literally left an impression on Lee. Tommy Wright, who came on for stricken Everton team-mate Newton, also suffered Mocanu's excessive attentions, but survived for what was fully expected to be the toughest test of the tournament – a meeting with Brazil and the great Pelé leading a cast of stars like Jairzinho, Rivelino and Tostão.

From day one in Mexico, England had faced hostility from many in the host nation. It was said that steaks imported on England's behalf for the tournament were impounded by Mexican officials, the story being that they represented a risk due to the outbreak of foot and mouth disease in UK cattle in 1967. Frozen fish was approved by the authorities, but was hardly an acceptable substitute for the prime cuts. On the eve of the Brazil game, the Hilton Hotel in Guadalajara, where England were staying, was besieged. Car horns blared and the noise was maintained into the early hours. The sense, of course, was that the locals were doing their utmost to disrupt England's preparations for a match that was to assume legendary status in the annals of football.

Back home, colour television – still something of a novelty at the time – brought an extra element of magic to the occasion, with the gleaming gold shirts of Brazil and brilliant white of England radiating in the scorching heat. In the match itself, which was accompanied by a classic commentary from David Coleman on the BBC, England started positively, keeping possession and probing the frailties of Brazil keeper Félix.

But Brazil's ability to suddenly find another gear was illustrated when captain Carlos Alberto played a long ball inside Cooper. The Leeds defender was no slouch, but neither was Jairzinho who sped outside him and raced to centre from the byline. The ball was high to the back post where Pelé was hanging in the air. He screamed 'gol!' as he connected with a downward header, but had reckoned without the agility and reflexes of Banks, who performed what was hailed as 'The Save of the Century' after switching his attention swiftly from the near post to the far to fling himself down and scoop the ball over the angle of upright and bar.

It was a miraculous stop and an ever-modest Banks, who was at the peak of his powers in 1970, recalled one of football's most memorable moments when he spoke to *FourFourTwo* magazine in 2016. He said, 'It was just instinct. You can't anticipate a header because your body weight would be all wrong, but in training beforehand I had Bobby Charlton hitting shots into the ground because the pitches were rock hard in Mexico. That helped me predict the bounce, but I honestly thought it had gone in. I looked around and said to myself, "Banksie, you lucky t***."' It was not the only save that Banks had to make to thwart Brazil, but it was by far the best.

In a game that was a lot more physical than most remember, Lee was the target for a show of Brazilian aggression after a challenge on Félix. The Manchester City man brought a save from the keeper with a diving header on the end of Wright's centre and when the ball looked to be breaking free, Lee attempted a follow-up, but only succeeded in kicking the grounded Félix as he gathered. Lee was immediately confronted by furious opponents and when Bobby Charlton tried a little diplomacy, he received a sharp shove from Carlos Alberto. Retribution was not long in coming as a forward run by Lee ended abruptly with Carlos Alberto's cynical body-check.

Yet this particular duel in the sun will always be characterised by its iconic moments and it also produced one of the greatest tackles of all time in the second half, when the immaculate Moore stopped Jairzinho in his tracks just inside England's penalty area. The timing was evidence of the captain's superb reading of the game.

It was Jairzinho, however, who undid England on the hour. Tostão used his forearm to fend off Ball – the type of challenge that would not evade scrutiny in the modern game – and was then fortunate again to nutmeg Moore before turning to pull the ball across. The centre fell at the feet of Pelé, who trapped the ball and it laid off on the right of the 18-yard box for Jairzinho to ram home past Banks. It was the solitary goal of an heroic struggle. England toiled to draw level, centre-forward Astle, who had come on as a substitute for Lee, missing a great chance to equalise when he shot wide with the goal at his mercy following the gift of a miskick in the Brazil defence. As England resorted to pumping long balls and crosses up to the West Bromwich Albion target man to exploit the uncertainty in the air of the suspect Félix all they could, Astle's knock-back found Ball whose shot glanced off the bar. An abiding post-match image is that of Moore and Pelé, face to face in a near-embrace as they swap shirts in a demonstration of warmth and mutual admiration. To England's credit, it was the only time a brilliant Brazil – regarded by many as the greatest team ever – scored fewer than three goals in any game during the tournament. Their 4-1 victory against Italy in the final in Mexico City's Estadio Azteca would confirm them as worthy world champions.

Brazil had begun with a win over Czechoslovakia by an identical result, and Ramsey rang the changes for England's final group game against the same opposition. England also had a new look with an all-sky-blue third-choice strip. World Cup winner Jack Charlton made his only appearance of the tournament – and his last in an England shirt – in place of Labone at the heart of defence alongside Moore, while Astle and Allan Clarke, on his debut, stood in for Lee and Hurst as Ramsey rested and nursed men after the stamina-sapping exchanges with Brazil. Three minutes into the second half, a foul on Colin Bell presented Clarke with the opportunity to slam home a penalty. Bell had a goal disallowed for offside and Ball's stinging strike hit the bar before England suffered a scare. Karol Dobiaš let fly and the shot seemed to swerve in the thin air and deceive Banks, who fumbled it on to the bar before recovering his composure. Bobby Charlton admitted, 'It was a bad game for us. There was so much tension about qualifying that we could not hit a thing right. The Czechs probably played better than us because they could have a crack without worrying.'

Ramsey came up with what was then a novel explanation for England's disappointing display. On a hot, sunny day at Southampton in 1996, Manchester United manager Alex Ferguson famously made his side change from grey shirts to dark blue and white at half-time as they headed for a 3-1 defeat, and 26 years earlier, Ramsey had a similar issue. He conceded he had 'made a mistake' with his choice of a 'pale blue' strip for his side, adding, 'In the sunlight, it was often impossible for our players to distinguish our shirts from the white of the Czechs.'

But there was no quick change of kit for England and Clarke's spot kick was enough for the win and a quarter-final date with destiny against West Germany. Banks was the best possible insurance policy England had, but there was no indemnity against illness and when 'Montezuma's Revenge' – as tummy trouble is known to those who visit Mexico – forced him out of the game, Bonetti had to step in, and the Germans perhaps sensed vengeance of their own.

As it was almost four years earlier, when England had led 2-1 before West Germany's late equaliser, extra time was required. But whereas in winning the most important game of their lives England had managed to grow in strength and belief in the additional half an hour after Ramsey's 'you've won the cup once, now go and win it again' pep talk, in Mexico (sides from northern Europe were not helped by midday kick-offs to suit television schedules) they visibly wilted in the searing temperature. It was still difficult to comprehend after Ramsey's boys had cruised into a 2-0 lead through Alan Mullery's forceful near-post finish after half an hour and Peters's untidy far-post effort five minutes into the second period, both stemming from crosses by hardworking right-back Newton. Many blamed Ramsey's decision to substitute Bobby Charlton, Bell taking his place. There was no doubt that the switch released Franz Beckenbauer to wield much more influence on the game, though he had already pulled a goal back in the 68th minute moments before Charlton was controversially withdrawn in what was his 106th and last international appearance, bettering the record of former England captain Billy Wright.

Beckenbauer's shot flew underneath Bonetti who, to be fair, then made a vital save to deny Gerd Müller. But in the 82nd minute, Bonetti was left stranded by a flukey Uwe Seeler back header that looped over the keeper's head and into the far corner of the net. Extra time arrived, West Germany coach Helmut Schön introduced Jürgen Grabowski, and a whole new threat emerged as the winger began to torment tiring left-back Cooper. The fatal blow was dealt in the 108th minute and it came from Grabowski's right-wing centre. Hannes Löhr headed the ball back across goal and Müller – aka *Der Bomber* – volleyed home from close range past a totally exposed Bonetti. Like Charlton, the Chelsea keeper would never play for England again.

The heartbreaking result prompted some to prematurely suggest that Ramsey's days as manager were numbered. His prickly relationship with sections of the press and media fed into that debate and he protested bitterly that he was accused of rudeness and yet had to endure microphones being thrust at his face with irritating regularity. In reality, Ramsey's future was never really up for discussion at that stage, but the winds of change among the playing ranks were blowing by the time England returned to action in a 3-1 friendly win against East Germany at Wembley in November in their final outing of 1970.

Ramsey handed Shilton a debut as Banks was given a well-earned breather. In East Germany's first visit to Wembley and one of only four all-time encounters with England, Lee struck in the 12th minute, racing on to Hurst's flick-on and rounding keeper Jürgen Croy to score. Peters made it 2-0 after 20 minutes with a deflected shot from the edge of the 18-yard box, but the visitors surprised England seven minutes later when Eberhard Vogel hit a venomous, long-range effort that left Shilton well beaten. England's two-goal cushion was restored, however, in the 63rd minute when Lee played in Clarke, who lofted the ball over Croy to complete the scoring.

A year that had proved traumatic for the footballing nation had ended on a winning note, but in truth, England's problems were only just beginning.

2

West Germany Calling Again

WALTER WINTERBOTTOM may have been England's first full-time manager in name but it was his successor, Alf Ramsey, who successfully redefined the role. During his 16 years in charge, Winterbottom was responsible for coaching and preparing the team, but selection was done by committee. It was only in the latter years of his tenure that he began to exert genuine influence over the Football Association's panel of selectors.

That, at least, laid the foundations for Ramsey – regarded by many as England's first real manager – to demand and command a broader remit: it was he who would pick the team. In a lot of respects, he was the perfect choice for the revised managerial post when his appointment was confirmed in October 1962. After all, as a Tottenham Hotspur right-back, who began his career with Southampton, Ramsey had played for England under Winterbottom and been through the mill, with the international side having suffered the humiliation of a 1-0 defeat at the hands of the United States at the 1950 World Cup in Belo Horizonte, Brazil, and been on the receiving end of the seismic 6-3 Wembley drubbing by Hungary three years later; in what was his 32nd and last game for his country, he scored his third goal. More importantly,

Ramsey – nicknamed 'The General' – had already proved his management credentials. Long before Brian Clough won a third-place promotion with Nottingham Forest in 1977 followed by the First Division championship a year later, Ramsey led an equally unfashionable Ipswich Town to the Second and First Division titles in 1961 and 1962, a staggering achievement.

Hailing from Dagenham in Essex and dismissive when asked about what was said to be his Romany background, Ramsey was to bring stolid stability to the England setup. Perceived as aloof and certainly taciturn by nature, he was nevertheless forthright. When pressed after his appointment to look ahead to England's prospects as hosts of the 1966 World Cup, he declared, 'England will win the World Cup.' Many thought the new man was making himself a hostage to fortune, but they were reckoning without Ramsey's unflinching resolve to deliver on what appeared to be a bold prediction. The doubters had reason to maintain their reservations, however, as England began Ramsey's reign with a failure. After Winterbottom, who resigned having taken England to four World Cup tournaments, had overseen an uninspiring 1-1 European Championship qualifying draw with France at Sheffield Wednesday's Hillsborough, Ramsey was at the helm in February 1963 for a deflating 5-2, second-leg defeat to the French at the Parc des Princes in Paris, which saw elimination from the competition. Just for good measure, Scotland then came to Wembley and won 2-1 in the annual encounter.

But Ramsey, whose loyalty to a by-then struggling Ipswich had seen him continue to work for the Suffolk club throughout much of the 1962/63 season, in which they secured First Division safety, was soon solely focused on transforming England's fortunes. Key decisions were taken, like the naming of a 22-year-old Bobby Moore as England's youngest captain in only his 12th appearance as he stood in for Jimmy Armfield in a 4-2 win in Czechoslovakia. Moore would later make the mantle his own and, of course, become England's most famous and successful skipper. It was full-on friendlies and British Home Championship matches in the build-up to the World Cup and the immortalisation of Moore and company. France were among England's victims at Wembley during the tournament as Ramsey made good on his prophecy.

* * *

By early 1971, with the loss of their crown in Mexico the previous summer still fresh in the mind, England were on a path of renewal and hoped-for redemption and Ramsey stepped up his experimentation as they headed into qualifying for the 1972 European Championship, his line-up showing seven changes to the one that started against West Germany in León. But they were to find the shadow of their old rivals inescapable.

England were in a comfortable-looking group alongside Switzerland, the most testing opposition, Greece and minnows Malta. A distinctly underwhelming 1-0 success against Malta in Valletta, with Martin Peters scoring ten minutes before half-time, marked England's first post-World Cup match in competition. Gordon Banks was back in goal as Derby County centre-back Roy McFarland, Tottenham striker Martin Chivers, Everton frontman Joe Royle and his Toffees team-mate, midfielder Colin Harvey, were all selected for the first – and in Harvey's case only – time. Alan Mullery skippered England in the absence of Moore after 1971 had begun with more trouble for the captain. West Ham, managed by future England boss Ron Greenwood, had disciplined Moore and others for a drinks outing on the eve of their FA Cup third-round tie at Blackpool. Moore,

Jimmy Greaves, Brian Dear and Clyde Best, having been led to believe the game would be called off due to a frozen pitch, headed out to former heavyweight boxer Brian London's nightclub.

But the quartet were spotted, the game went ahead and, after the Hammers suffered a 4-0 hammering and the story emerged of the ill-advised social excursion, there were consequences for those involved. With Moore in the team at Bloomfield Road, gifted Scot Tony Green – who would face England at the end of that season in the British Home Championship – was the architect of the demise of Greenwood's men. Armfield, Moore's predecessor as England captain, was in the Blackpool side that day.

Moore felt he and his team-mates had been hung out to dry and later admitted that his relationship with West Ham and Greenwood was never the same again. Ramsey recalled Moore for England's next game in April, a 3-0 victory over Greece at Wembley, where Arsenal defender Peter Storey made his bow – and the third goal of the night. A pass by Peters was deflected into the path of Chivers, who used all his strength to work his way in on the left to smash home the opener after 23 minutes. But the home crowd had to hang on until 20 minutes from time to see England go further in front. The ball travelled from left to right as Francis Lee's cross was only partially cleared and picked up by Peters, who chipped into the box where Chivers flicked on and Geoff Hurst's header looped beyond Nikos Christidis in the Greece goal. As England stepped up the pressure, Hurst was impeded as the Greeks' defending became niggly and he was awarded a free kick. Mullery whipped it in quickly and the keeper's reactions were razor-sharp as he touched Peters's header on to the bar and then held on to a follow-up effort by Chivers. But a third goal was only a matter of time and, three minutes from the end, Storey crossed on the right and Lee was lurking in the middle to glance home.

The reverse fixture with Malta was more like it from England, a 5-0 demolition job with Chivers netting twice and taking his haul to three in two games as Ramsey introduced Chris Lawler to the senior international stage. The dependable Liverpool right-back did not disappoint, crashing in England's fifth goal in the 74th minute from around 30 yards with a terrific strike. Chivers launched the rout in the first minute when he glanced in a Peters free kick that was floated to the near post. Lee added the second five minutes from the interval with a header from a Peters knock-down. Allan Clarke netted a penalty for handball within moments of the restart after the break and Chivers wasted no time in making it 4-0 on 47 minutes. It was a slick move as Lee found Peters on the right and it was another goal made in Tottenham as the radar-like cross was met by the head of the climbing Chivers.

A distraction from the European qualifying campaign came with the British Home Championship, which provided a very rare moment of embarrassment for Banks. The culprit was Northern Ireland superstar George Best and the incident caused uproar at Belfast's Windsor Park. Best faced Banks as he clutched the ball, preparing to clear from his penalty area. Convention had it that Best's pressure tactic would be followed by Banks stepping aside and hoofing the ball upfield. Best, though, was never one for convention. As Banks swayed to his left to deliver the intended clearance, Best stuck out an impudent leg to play the ball as soon as it had left the keeper's hands and hook it goalward. Best then ran on to the ball to head into an unguarded goal. Amid much finger-wagging on England's part, Scottish referee Alistair MacKenzie ruled the goal out on the grounds of dangerous play by Best.

Northern Ireland's sense of grievance was compounded when Liam O'Kane's ball was charged down by what looked like the hand of Lee, who released Clarke to score the only goal of a game that saw Paul Madeley finally make it into Ramsey's side. England then drew 0-0 with Wales at Wembley, where Liverpool hard man Tommy Smith and West Bromwich Albion striker Tony Brown won their only caps, while Anfield centre-back Larry Lloyd, later of Nottingham Forest, made the first of just four appearances for his country spanning, remarkably, nine years. England regained the championship outright with a 3-1 triumph over Scotland, a game played with an orange ball similar to the one used in the World Cup Final five years earlier. A change of ball – but not colour – was required, however, in the opening moments of Scotland's visit to Wembley after doubts about its quality were aired to Dutch referee Jef Dorpmans. Despite that disruption, the match still produced a frenetic and rather bizarre start when Peters gave England the lead after nine minutes. Alan Ball released Lee down the line on the right and England's number seven won a corner. It was Ball who took it and when Chivers flicked on, the header by Peters was fisted on to the bar by John Greig, who was positioned on the goal line. It was demonstrable that the whole of the ball had not crossed the line, but Dorpmans awarded the goal and Scotland's reaction to what should have been a highly controversial decision was strangely muted as they could have argued far more vigorously that it ought to have been a penalty.

As it turned out, they were soon on level terms through Wolves striker Hugh Curran. Ball headed back towards goal under pressure and Curran, who was played onside, appeared to get the faintest of touches with his right foot as Banks bore down on him. Chivers's purple patch then continued as he struck twice to put England in control by the break. On the half-hour mark, Lee bravely won two challenges and the ball broke kindly for Chivers to thunder in a left-footed drive from around 25 yards. Then, two minutes before the interval,

Lawler helped the ball on for Chivers to chip keeper Bobby Clark in delightful style for his second goal. Peters fluffed a good chance to extend England's lead after the break, but ten minutes into a much quieter second half, Spurs team-mate Chivers was denied a hat-trick. Terry Cooper crossed from the left and Hurst glanced on for Chivers to finish at the far post. But in the days when an attacking player being level with the last opposition defender meant he was offside, the powerful frontman was frustrated in his attempt to emulate strike partner Hurst by netting a treble for England under the Twin Towers.

Qualifying for the European Championship resumed in October with a 3-2 victory in Switzerland, where England only edged the win with an own goal by defender Anton Weibel inside the last quarter of an hour after leading twice early in the game through Hurst and Chivers. For Hurst, there were shades of 1966. As against West Germany, when famously there were doubts about his second goal being over the line, it was questionable whether Hurst's header in the opening moments in Basel had crossed the line as keeper Marcel Kunz got his hands on the ball low down at the near post. After Daniel Jeandupeux levelled in the tenth minute, Chivers netted in the 12th, but the Swiss equalised again just before the break with a goal by Fritz Künzli. So, in the end, England were grateful for Weibel's wobble.

When the Swiss came to Wembley a month later, colourful Queens Park Rangers forward Rodney Marsh made his England breakthrough as a substitute in a disappointing 1-1 draw. His future Manchester City team-mate, Mike Summerbee, scored his only goal in an England shirt with a looping header in the ninth minute after a centre by Emlyn Hughes had popped up invitingly from Switzerland's failure to deal with the dangerous delivery. England's own shortcomings were punished, though, when Switzerland skipper Karl Odermatt hit back after 25 minutes with a power-packed strike, on the right corner of the penalty area, that carried such pace that it eluded the grasp of Peter Shilton at his near upright. Ramsey admitted, 'We will have to play a lot better than in this game and the other against Switzerland if we are to progress to the final. They played very well. They made it terribly difficult to score and often had eight men in defence. Basically, their pattern of play was to stop England scoring. I think what probably upset me most was our failure to pass accurately. I dare not try to count the number of times we gave the ball away.'

But the Hurst-Chivers combo did the trick again in a 2-0 December win against Greece, who were by then under the stewardship of Northern Ireland legend Billy Bingham. At the Karaiskakis Stadium in Piraeus, Athens, England secured their passage to the quarter-finals of the European Championship. Hurst hammered in a goal on the hour and Chivers struck in the last minute, but the margin of the win should have been much greater, with Lee hitting the woodwork twice.

A sense of déjà vu then descended on Ramsey and his men as West Germany loomed large again in the new year. Wembley, where England had prevailed over the Germans to win the ultimate prize, staged something of a curiosity in those days – a Saturday night match. And the evening, with a Wembley surface given extra zip by April showers, belonged to one man: Günter Netzer. Not a familiar name to England fans at the time perhaps, but one they would never forget after this pivotal encounter. Netzer was a marauding midfielder with long, blond hair and skills to match his striking appearance. It was also a game in which Moore made mistakes that would, sadly, become more common and costly as his England career began to wane.

The skipper turned into trouble in his own area and gave the ball away before Uli Hoeneß handed West Germany the lead after 25 minutes with a drive from the edge of the area. Lee hauled the home side back into the game with 12 minutes to go, tapping into an empty net from close range after Manchester City team-mate Colin Bell's shot had been met with a poor parry by Sepp Maier. Then, in a fevered four minutes, the Germans took the game away from England. A breakaway by the visitors in the 84th minute ended with Moore bringing down Siggi Held – a survivor of West Germany's 1966 team – inside the box. Moore got a toe on the ball as he made the challenge but caught the forward with his follow-through. Netzer netted the resultant penalty, Banks pushing the ball on to a post on its way in.

And Gerd Müller, England's executioner in Mexico, delivered the *coup de grâce* once more just two minutes from time with a shot that scraped away from Banks and in off the same upright after tired left-back Hughes had lost the ball. For Hurst, hat-trick hero against the Germans in 1966, it was an international swansong.

At 'An Evening With Sir Geoff Hurst' at Darlington's Hippodrome Theatre in March 2023, part of a countrywide tour promoted by A1 Sporting Speakers, Hurst hailed the 'backbone' of the England teams he played in at the 1966 and 1970 World Cups. He said, 'We had Banksie, the best goalkeeper in the world, Mooro, immaculate, a great leader and a great reader of the game, and Bobby [Charlton] in midfield – 49 goals in 106 games for England, not far off a goal every two games.' Indeed, Hurst had such admiration for West Ham and England team-mate Moore that he admitted he was his 'sporting hero' and 'idol', even though, as he stressed, his captain 'was only eight months older' than him.

The early 1970s was a curious time for Moore: there were the controversies of Bogotá and Blackpool and, in January 1972, he stepped in as an emergency goalkeeper for West Ham in their epic League Cup semi-final with Stoke. In a second replay at Old Trafford, keeper Bobby Ferguson was forced to leave the field for treatment and, during his absence, Moore saved a penalty from one-time England under-23 international Mike Bernard, only for the midfielder to score from the rebound. Banks, who had been beaten by a penalty from Hurst in the first leg of the semi-final, saved brilliantly to keep out his England colleague's spot kick in the second leg at Upton Park and help Stoke to a 1-0 win after extra time on the night, tying the aggregate score at 2-2 and leading to what turned out to be a further three and a half hours of drama. Stoke eventually prevailed and beat Chelsea in the final and, at the start of the following season, Hurst would join Banks in the Potteries after the England keeper had convinced him it was the right move.

* * *

The defeat by West Germany was England's first at Wembley since the delirious Scots had partied five years earlier and it was the heaviest loss on home soil in Ramsey's reign. It carried echoes of the humbling by Hungary in 1953, when the Magical Magyars eclipsed the country that had given football to the world.

For Helmut Schön's West Germany, who would go on to become European champions by beating the Soviet Union in Brussels, the comprehensive victory over England was effectively mission accomplished in terms of reaching the last four. England's fate was duly confirmed after a goalless draw in the teeming Berlin rain two weeks later when Marsh was their first new starter in almost a calendar year and performed well enough to convince Ramsey he was worth a run in the side.

It was Ramsey's deployment of defensive-minded hard men Storey and Norman Hunter in midfield that drew the most attention, however, as Schön led a chorus of condemnation, branding England's tackling as 'brutal'. Ramsey also came under fire from elements of the English press who were uncomfortable with what were viewed as strong-arm tactics. The reasoning behind Ramsey's selection was clear, though. Having been torn apart by Netzer at Wembley, England needed more mettle to counter that particular threat. After the Berlin encounter, Netzer quipped that every England player had autographed his leg. As it transpired, he still managed to go closer than anyone else to scoring, albeit from a long-range free kick that slammed against the crossbar. In a tedious, niggly contest, the Germans – marshalled by the consummate authority of skipper Franz Beckenbauer – were largely content to contain England, for whom Chivers was a threat. Both Beckenbauer and Netzer reacted angrily to some of England's tough tackling, but in the end, the added steel in the engine room was not strong enough to break a resolute German side.

3

Changing of the Guard

NEWCASTLE UNITED'S powerful and pacy striker Malcolm Macdonald lined up to make his England debut when Sir Alf Ramsey's side returned to action, only a week after drowning in Berlin's downpour, with a welcome 3-0 British Home Championship win against Wales at Cardiff.

Emlyn Hughes and Rodney Marsh were among the goals for the first time, with the outstanding Colin Bell also on the scoresheet. On a threadbare Ninian Park pitch, England took the lead in the 25th minute when the rampaging and effervescent Hughes combined with Marsh to start the move – and finish it. Macdonald helped the ball on for Bell, whose shot was spilled by Gary Sprake and left-back Hughes was on hand to tuck away from close range. There were scares for England, though, before they went on to establish their authority. Gordon Banks saved from striker John Toshack, but also had a very unusual lapse when he failed to deal with a dangerous free kick which flashed across the face of goal from right-back Peter Rodrigues. In the second half, the vigilance of Bobby Moore was vital as he blocked the header of striker Ron Davies near the goal line, but after seeing an offside flag end his celebrations when he thought for a moment he had broken his duck for his country, Marsh did just that in the 69th minute with a supreme finish. Peter Storey hoisted the ball up to Macdonald, whose knock-back was met by Marsh's first-time strike which sped past the helpless Sprake. Moments later, Mike Summerbee crossed for Manchester City colleague Bell to hook home and cap an integral midfield display.

But it was only a temporary confidence booster as Northern Ireland, whose traditional strip of green shirts and white shorts was similar to the change colours worn by West Germany against England the previous month, inflicted back-to-back Wembley defeats on Ramsey's side. It was the first time that had happened to England in 21 years and just the second occasion in their history. Northern Ireland player-manager Terry Neill scored the only goal of the game. When England lost to West Germany, there were five members – Banks, Moore, Geoff Hurst, Alan Ball and Martin Peters – of the World Cup winners in the starting line-up. Against Northern Ireland, there were none. Peters did appear as a substitute, coming on for Sheffield United's midfield debutant Tony Currie, while Derby County defender Colin Todd also won his first cap.

As Ramsey strove to give England a new identity, he showed his stubborn streak and tried to make a point to his critics against Scotland by naming the same, unpopular side that had started in the second leg with the Germans. Ball, complete with his by-then trademark – though somewhat grey-looking – white boots, scored the only goal of a hard-earned win in Glasgow. Rarely did things come easily to England at Hampden Park and Ramsey was never under any illusions about the reception that awaited them. On arrival at Prestwick Airport for their British Home Championship clash in 1968, Ramsey had dropped his normally mannerly demeanour. 'Welcome to Scotland, Sir Alf,' said a Scottish reporter. 'You must be f****** joking,' replied Ramsey.

England were always right to feel embattled when they took on the Scots, especially north of the border. In 1972, seemingly inspired by the cunning trick George Best had played on Banks a year earlier, Scotland appeared keen to rattle the England keeper with similarly claustrophobic attention. When right-back John Brownlie sent over a deep centre, Banks had to claim it under the crossbar and the waspish duo of Denis Law and Lou Macari swarmed around him. Banks was quick with a retaliatory barge on Macari after the Celtic forward had charged into him on the goal line.

Banks looked less than sure of himself as he cleared at the second attempt from the feet of Peter Lorimer, and Storey had to knock off the line to deny Asa Hartford, but England broke the deadlock when Billy Bremner lost possession to Ball who was on the end of a well-worked move to bundle in a finish that trickled home. Bell should have doubled the lead before the interval but hit a post with his shot after being set up by Martin Chivers.

In the second period, a cheeky Scottish fan ran on to the pitch with a bunch of flowers for England – and Norman Hunter hurled the ironic floral tribute towards the touchline. It needed Hughes to hack away on the line when Law connected with a downward header and England kept their lead intact. There was an increasing feeling, however, that they were starting to drift and a share of the British Home Championship title did little to alleviate the mood of unease. The significance of that game at Hampden would later dawn on the nation following shocking events on 22 October 1972, when sadness and despair descended on the world of football.

From an England perspective, the month began with Joe Royle scoring his first goal for his country in a 1-1 friendly draw at home to Yugoslavia, against whom new caps were handed to full-backs Mick Mills and Frank Lampard, centre-back Jeff Blockley and forward Mick Channon in a game which served as a warm-up for the start of World Cup qualifying the following month. Blockley's cap, which turned out to be the only one he won despite a decent display, came in the week after he had completed a £200,000 move from Coventry City to Arsenal. Ipswich Town right-back Mills would have to hang on for another three and a half years for the second of his 42 caps in a near-ten-year England career which would take him to the 1982 World Cup, while West Ham left-back Lampard endured an even longer wait – over seven and a half years – for his only other appearance.

The Yugoslavs were skippered by skilful winger Dragan Džajić, scorer of the goal that beat England in the 1968 European Championship semi-final before Italy prevailed in the final after the hosts had gone through farcically on a coin toss following a goalless draw against the Soviet Union. With the vastly experienced Džajić pulling the strings in a record 66th appearance for his country, a quick, slick Yugoslavia provided a searching test for an experimental England line-up.

There was a warning when Peter Shilton, deputising for Banks, needed to make a sharp save to deny debutant Franjo Vladić an opening goal. Channon's chip threatened a similar outcome when Enver Marić tipped over. The keeper, however, suffered a rush of blood six minutes before half-time as he charged out on the right side of his goal, giving Channon the chance to capitalise. His cross was poor, but not as bad as the defending, and the chaos presented the alert Ball with the opportunity to square his pass to the unmarked Royle, who rammed home a powerful shot.

But Yugoslavia were level five minutes into the second period and, this time, schemer Vladić's luck was in as he popped up behind the England defence to nod in from forward Dušan Bajević's knock-down on the end of a deep centre by right-back Petar Krivokuća. England's appeals for offside were futile, and they were punished for that offence themselves when Ball then volleyed in after Bell's right-wing corner had broken loose. It was the sweetest of connections by Ball, but Marsh was in an offside position and in the eye line of keeper Marić. In truth, the technically gifted Yugoslavs always looked the more likely winners. Shilton pulled off a fine, flying save from Vladić's strike, Bajević fired into the side netting and then Džajić hit the bar with a chip after realising the England keeper was off his line.

When World Cup qualifying began for England with another trip to Wales, it was Ray Clemence, not Shilton, who was between the posts. And so began their tussle to be England's number one and fill an almighty void which had unexpectedly opened up only 11 days after the Yugoslavia game. On his way home after undergoing treatment for an injury following Stoke's 2-1 defeat away to Liverpool the day before, Banks was involved in an horrific car crash on a narrow country road. He was rushed to hospital where he underwent extensive and intricate surgery for eye and head injuries. Due to the shower of shards of glass from the shattered windscreen of his vehicle, his right eye had sustained serious damage. Pictures of a bed-bound Banks, with a patch over his eye and stitches on his forehead, horrified a nation who held him in such high regard and affection. The chances of Banks being able to see again out of his right eye hung in the balance.

He was inundated with letters and cards expressing support, sympathy and good wishes. A comeback was hoped for but, ultimately, all vision in his right eye was lost. Yet a defiant Banks was playing again six months later, albeit in an unofficial international match. Ramsey took an FA XI, which also included Banks's fellow World Cup winner Nobby Stiles, to Gibraltar where they won 9-0. Banks captained the side, but both he and Stiles were substituted at half-time. Frank Worthington scored a hat-trick and a young Trevor Francis netted twice.

Banks returned to Stoke, managed by Tony Waddington, after his lay-off, but he knew they were merely delaying the inevitable. At the end of the 1972/73 season, he was forced to accept that his playing days in England – and for England after amassing 73 caps – were over at the age of 35. A year earlier, he had won the coveted Football Writers' Association Player of the Year award and had once again been a winner in a Wembley final, this time with Stoke in their League Cup victory over Chelsea. Naturally anxious to do all he could to help, Waddington handed Banks the position of youth-team coach, but he longed for a return to playing. The chance to do so eventually came his way when North American Soccer League side Fort Lauderdale Strikers approached him in 1976. It was a gamble but one that paid off. Banks proved – admittedly at a lower standard of football than he had obviously been accustomed to yet in a league which was competitive enough – he was still a very capable keeper despite his disability. It was in 1979, seven years after the accident that changed his life, that he finally hung up his gloves.

Shilton's career, at least initially, followed an uncannily similar path to Banks: he succeeded him as first-choice keeper at Leicester – and in time with England – and then joined Stoke where Banks had headed after leaving the Foxes. Speaking to Sky Sports after the death of Banks at the age of 81 on 12 February 2019, Shilton said, 'Gordon was my hero when I was a youngster watching Leicester on the terraces and I eventually joined the club and became his understudy at 16. I trained with him for about a year and he was always helpful and always a gentleman. He was a great goalkeeper. Of course, when you have worked with Gordon, it's bound to rub off on you a little bit and I always admired his positional play. It was a different era for goalkeepers with different rules, but it was still the same job – keeping the ball out of the net.'

The England team that Banks had once graced commenced their campaign to reach the 1974 World Cup in West Germany with a side containing only two of the stars of 1966 – Moore and Ball. Having qualified as hosts then holders for the previous two World Cups, there was precious little margin for error as Ramsey's men had to finish top of a three-team group, which as well as Wales also featured Poland, to secure qualification. England may have been favourites to progress from their section, but the start they made in November 1972 was rather inauspicious, a 1-0 win over Wales through Bell's 35th-minute goal as he again made the most of a visit at Ninian Park, where future captain and manager Kevin Keegan debuted.

Clemence retained his place for the return clash at Wembley two months later, but it was here that England began to stumble. Moore won his 99th cap in England's first World Cup game beneath the Twin Towers since he had lifted the trophy there six and a half years earlier. There was another England playing that night – for Wales. Tottenham defender Mike England was Moore's opposing captain.

Having made England work for their win at Cardiff, Wales were never going to be pushovers and, with little to lose, they took the game to their hosts. Leighton James burst through on the left to test Clemence with a near-post shot that the keeper could only parry for a corner. But when the tricky Burnley winger then appeared on the opposite flank in the 23rd minute and pulled the ball back from the byline, he presented Clemence's unmarked Liverpool team-mate Toshack with the simplest of close-range tap-ins into an unguarded goal. The tension at Wembley was tangible as Wales impressed and England struggled. Chivers came agonisingly close to equalising before Hunter produced a 30-yard screamer three minutes from the break to beat his Leeds colleague Sprake in the Wales goal. Level at the interval, England pressed hard for a winner that never materialised, Marsh's header against the bar the closest they came to leading.

If England needed a pick-me-up, it came the following month – 14 February, to be precise – with a resounding 5-0 win over Scotland, predictably dubbed the St Valentine's Day Massacre, on a wintry night and a snow-flecked Hampden Park pitch in a game to mark the centenary of the Scottish FA. There was a ton-up milestone for England, too, with Moore making his 100th appearance for his country. Southampton forward Channon was recalled to win his second England cap and opened his goal account after quarter of an hour, while Allan Clarke played for his country for the first time in nearly two years and sent Ramsey a message with a double strike, his first coming in the 12th minute and the second five minutes from the end. There was also a very rare item to start the ball rolling – a sixth-minute own goal by Clarke's Leeds team-mate, Lorimer. Chivers registered, too, in the 76th minute, leaving Ramsey so impressed with his scorers that he made them his preferred front three up to, and including, the last knockings of the World Cup qualifying campaign. But before England renewed their rivalry with the Scots and Wales in the British Home Championship, the Welsh well and truly put the cat among the pigeons when they produced a fine 2-0 victory over Poland in a March qualifier in Cardiff.

England went into the Home Championship with an away game – on home soil. Everton's Goodison Park staged what should have been a visit to Belfast to face Northern Ireland. The game was switched to Liverpool due to The Troubles in the province as the fallout continued from Bloody Sunday in January 1972, when British troops opened fire during civil rights demonstrations in the predominantly Catholic Bogside area of Londonderry/Derry, ultimately leading to the deaths of 14 people. Scotland had been due to play Northern Ireland in

Belfast that year in the Home Championship but after death threats were made to the Scots by Irish Republicans, the match was rescheduled to Hampden. The threats lingered in 1973, forcing Northern Ireland to abandon their traditional home again. So Goodison, which also hosted Northern Ireland's 'home' game with Wales, witnessed a 2-1 win for England, Chivers scoring twice. The first goal, in the ninth minute, followed an unfamiliar error by his Spurs team-mate, keeper Pat Jennings, who juggled the ball in at the near post after Chivers had met Ball's free kick with a header. The Irish levelled when Sheffield Wednesday's Dave Clements – on what would become his home ground when he moved to Everton later that year – dispatched a 23rd-minute penalty that was too good for Shilton, but Chivers made the most of uncertain defending in the 82nd minute to round Jennings and slot home. Wolves striker John Richards glanced the ball on to Chivers from a delivery by fellow debutant David Nish. While the Derby County left-back went on to win four more caps, it was, inexplicably, the last seen of Richards – who was a prolific scorer for his club – in an England shirt. It was a below-par performance from Ramsey's side, who were barracked by sections of the crowd, but they then produced the sort of result against Wales at Wembley that they could have done with when the sides had met there four months earlier.

A thorough 3-0 victory was chiefly down to the effective front three of Chivers, Channon and Clarke. Centre-forward Chivers opened the scoring in the 23rd minute with a beautifully controlled volley from around the edge of the penalty area, the bounce of the ball offering Welsh keeper John Phillips – Peter Bonetti's understudy at Chelsea – little chance. Channon then underlined England's authority after half an hour, breaking down the right and going outside his man before hitting a shot just inside the far post. Peters supplied the third in the 66th minute with a first-time finish in front of goal, but Clarke missed out on one himself on the night in spite of his influential performance.

The manager named an unchanged side for the visit of Scotland four days later, when Peters struck again for the only goal of the game to secure the British crown with a clean sweep of victories. In a mainly unmemorable clash, the Scots had looked certain to go ahead early on when hot-shot Lorimer darted clear on the left but, thankfully for England, rounded off his run with a tame effort by his standards and Shilton was able to push the ball aside. After their Hampden hammering earlier in the year, Scotland were determined to give a good account of themselves and regain some pride against the Auld Enemy – and they did that. Clarke had the ball in the Scottish net but was adjudged offside and then missed a glorious opening. Ball's free kick was perfect for Chivers, but keeper Ally Hunter got both hands to the header to turn the ball over. After the break, however, Ball served up another free kick and this time Chivers was the decoy for Peters to live up to his nickname and 'Ghost' in at the far post to head in. Kenny Dalglish brought the best out of Shilton with a lavish half-volley that the keeper clawed away at full stretch, but Peters's 54th-minute goal was enough for England.

It soon became clear that Ramsey had decided on the nucleus of his side for the rest of the year leading up to the climax of the World Cup qualifying programme. Once defender Paul Madeley had returned to the side for a 1-1 friendly draw against Czechoslovakia in Prague – Leeds colleague Clarke levelling four minutes from time after Igor Novák's opener ten minutes into the second half – to hold down a place for the remainder of 1973, the team seemed to virtually pick itself. But Ramsey's faith in the chosen few would end up being misplaced.

4

Poles Apart

WHEN ENGLAND visited Poland for their World Cup qualifier on 6 June 1973, Sir Alf Ramsey's side included only three members of his all-conquering team of 1966 – captain Bobby Moore, Alan Ball and Martin Peters.

Amid a din of horns in the Stadion Śląski, Chorzów, on the outskirts of Katowice, England's every intervention in the early stages of the game was greeted with jeers from the hostile home fans. It might have been mid-summer, but behind the old Iron Curtain Ramsey's men, decked in an unfamiliar strip of yellow shirts, navy shorts and yellow socks, were caught cold and soon in trouble as the polished Poles went in front in only the seventh minute. Robert Gadocha drilled his left-wing free kick into the penalty area and Moore deflected the ball in off keeper Peter Shilton at the near post with Jan Banaś, who was lurking just behind the visiting skipper, claiming the goal.

A minute into the second half, Moore was found wanting again when he was much too lax as he tried to deal with the ball midway inside his own half and, turning inside, was robbed of possession by opposing captain Włodzimierz Lubański, who then sped clear to fire in off Shilton's near post. It was an unusual mistake by Moore, but it would have serious repercussions for his future as an England player. In truth, the back door always looked to be ajar in the England defence, in considerable contrast to the hosts who had the giant, blond-haired Jerzy Gorgoń at centre-back keeping any threat under lock and key for most of the match.

Lubański, who was reported to have a knee niggle going into the game, had shown little sign of labouring before he was forced off in the 54th minute after a challenge by Roy McFarland. But the nightmare worsened for England when Ball became only the second player in their history – Alan Mullery was the first against Yugoslavia in 1968 – to be sent off. The midfielder tangled with Lesław Ćmikiewicz in the 77th minute and Austrian referee Paul Schiller raised a straight red card. Ball reacted by momentarily going for Polish defender Krzysztof Rześny before thinking better of it. Poland had lacked influential attacker Grzegorz Lato, but it made no difference to the outcome. They banished, in emphatic fashion, the memory of their drubbing by Wales three months earlier and a ticket to West Germany for England a year hence suddenly looked a lot less assured.

On the back of their defeat in Poland, England faced another Eastern Bloc test against the Soviet Union in a friendly in the oppressive heat of Moscow where they won 2-1 with a Martin Chivers strike and an own goal by Murtaz Khurtsilava. It was an untidy opening goal after ten minutes when the perseverance of Chivers produced a dividend as he challenged two defenders to a high ball in the penalty area before lifting it beyond keeper Yevhen Rudakov. It was 2-0 ten minutes into the second half when Mick Channon's low, left-wing corner was turned goalward at the near post by the unfortunate Khurtsilava, with Rudakov only helping the ball in with a hand. Midfielder Volodymyr Muntyan reduced the arrears with a 66th-minute penalty after right-back Sergei

Olshansky went down rather too easily in a coming together with Peter Storey. The Soviets threatened an equaliser and had a goal disallowed. Muntyan, a big influence on the game, found Oleg Blokhin who broke into the box and squared the ball for substitute Vladimir Kozlov to poke home, but he was well offside and England held on for victory.

Malcolm Macdonald, who went on for Allan Clarke, recalled, 'I came on as a sub when we played at the Lenin Stadium, and the great Oleg Blokhin was playing for the Soviet Union. There was a huge crowd for an afternoon game and the first ten rows were taken up by the army. There was hardly any noise due to the presence of the army. But hostility was something we used to enjoy. We used to rub our hands and react to it in a positive way. The last thing it ever did was frighten us. We would think, "We're English, no one intimidates us."'

There was never any shortage of hostile reaction when England visited Italy, as they did in their next outing. Turin's Stadio Comunale was the setting for the *Azzurri* to taste victory over England for the first time, winning 2-0. It was not the way that Moore would have wanted to become his country's most-capped player outright as he eclipsed Bobby Charlton's record with his 107th appearance. When Pietro Anastasi opened the scoring in the 37th minute, his follow-up went through the legs of Moore on the goal line after Shilton had come out bravely to block the effort of Paolo Pulici. Future England boss Fabio Capello then grabbed the second goal seven minutes after the break, beating Shilton at his near post with the keeper getting a touch on the shot. It was a reminder of England's frailty against high-class opposition, but a 7-0 assault on Austria at Wembley three months later somewhat glossed over the loss to Italy and appeared to have provided an ideal platform for the crunch return encounter with Poland.

England simply ran riot, with Clarke and Channon sharing four goals and Chivers, Tony Currie and Colin Bell also chipping in. Pitiful Austria were powerless in the face of England's onslaught, which began in the tenth minute when Peters lifted the ball in from the right and Chivers and Channon challenged in the air, with the latter seemingly applying the final touch. A clinical Clarke then controlled Currie's far-post cross on his chest before rifling into the far corner of the net in the 27th minute. The Leeds striker scored another, two minutes before the break, after a fully extended Bell brilliantly kept an overhit ball in play to volley a centre for Clarke to tuck home at the second attempt from keeper Friedrich Koncilia's initial block.

Three minutes into the second period, Clarke's shot was fumbled against a post by Koncilia and, though there were suspicions that the ball had already crossed the line, what might have been a hat-trick became a brace for Channon, who raced in to bury the follow-up.

Currie crossed for Chivers's tap-in to make it 5-0 just after the hour mark. Then, three minutes later, Currie got in on the goalscoring act with his first for England, bringing the ball down on his chest and volleying in from just outside the 18-yard box before Bell drilled home two minutes from time to place the seal on the rout. While England dismantled the Austrians, the Poles upped the ante in World Cup qualifying by walloping Wales 3-0 in Chorzów, where midfielder Trevor Hockey suffered the same fate as Ball, and Gadocha, Lato and a certain Jan Domarski – a trio who would be back to haunt England – crushed the hopes of West Germany '74 for Dave Bowen's side.

When Poland arrived on 17 October for what was, for England, a must-win game, Wembley was a cauldron of expectation. Poland's idiosyncratic keeper Jan Tomaszewski was always going to be key to the outcome, but no one in their wildest dreams could have envisaged his impact. Brian Clough, speaking on the BBC's *World Cup Grandstand* before England's earlier match in Poland, had been scathing in his assessment of the Poles, branding them 'amateurs' and dismissing their prospects of making any impression in the push to reach the World Cup finals at the expense of the two home nations.

To say those words were ill-judged would be a gross understatement, but it was Clough's Wembley comments on Tomaszewski on 'the other side' – ITV, that was – which would command headlines. Clough labelled the keeper 'a circus clown in gloves' and stubbornly stuck to the line even in the post-match analysis. But on a night of slapstick farce, all the jokes were on an England side that again had one very notable absentee: Moore was omitted for the second successive game as Ramsey kept faith with the team that had hammered Austria. Lubański, who had picked Moore's pocket so damagingly in the first instalment, was missing through injury. Domarski, the man who had come on for the stricken Lubański in Chorzów, would take up his mantle at Wembley, though it was Tomaszewski who attracted all the attention.

The keeper was certainly unorthodox, as was illustrated in the opening minutes of the game. Poland conceded a free kick for a foul on Clarke, and Tomaszewski claimed Peters's set piece, which had been aimed for Chivers. Having seemingly dealt comfortably with any danger, Tomaszewski then attempted to roll the ball across goal but dropped it too heavily and nearly gifted a goal to Clarke, who had closed in quickly.

Tomaszewski recovered the situation, but in the process suffered an injury. Referee Vital Loraux, who had taken charge of England's game against Romania at the 1970 World Cup – the Belgian official was deemed to have been more than a little lenient in dealing with the tackling of the notorious Mihai Mocanu – initially ignored Tomaszewski's distress signals.

When the referee finally acknowledged there was a problem, the keeper received on-pitch treatment for what appeared to be a dislocated finger. While, at the time, most would have thought the offending digit had been snapped back into place, it later emerged that Tomaszewski had, in fact, splintered small bones in his wrist. That made his subsequent heroics and indefatigable defiance, albeit aided by the numbing effects of painkillers, all the more astounding. Another free kick by Peters, captaining England, was chipped to the far post where centre-back McFarland slid in to direct the ball into the goalmouth. But neither Chivers nor Channon could apply a finishing touch, the ball glancing off a post to safety from the Southampton favourite. England threatened again, a knock-down by Peters falling for Chivers, whose close-range shot was charged down. Currie and Channon both tried to pick up the pieces before the ball broke to Bell, who unloaded a venomous strike that was kept out by Tomaszewski's terrific full-length save. The technique was less convincing when Tomaszewski turned away Clarke's header for a corner, which the eccentric keeper failed to claim as we went walkabout in his area. But as the first half drew to a close, he then offered more evidence of his ability with an outstanding stop as he climbed to tip a Channon header over the bar.

Frustration mounted for a disbelieving home crowd after the half-time interval. There were cries of 'all we are saying, is give us a goal'. Currie blazed a great chance wide with only Tomaszewski to beat, but the Sheffield United star then hit a scorching drive that was palmed aside by the busiest man on the pitch before Channon followed up by smashing a volley into the side netting.

Then came the moment that undid England. Currie lost possession far too easily to Henryk Kasperczak, who fed the ball down the line for Lato, with Norman Hunter waiting. 'Bites Yer Legs' they called him, the Leeds defender never known for being shy about putting his foot into a challenge, but this time it was different. Hunter tentatively stepped on the ball rather than his man on the touchline on halfway. A grateful Lato nicked the ball and broke to cut in with Gadocha moving to his left. The better option, though, was to Lato's right where Domarski had made the run. Shilton was exposed, Emlyn Hughes's lunge for the ball was too late, but the keeper should have saved Domarski's near-post shot, which crept under his body. With 12 minutes gone in the second half, England were stunned, but time was still on their side. Ramsey's men soon rallied and almost immediately had the ball in the net themselves when Chivers delivered a long throw-in from the right, Peters jumped and Clarke laid the ball off for Channon who fired inside Tomaszewski's left-hand upright before Loraux ruled the goal out. The question was why? Was there a foul by Peters or Clarke? Harsh did not come close to a summing-up of the decision.

It was Peters who was brought down by Adam Musiał on the right edge of the penalty area when England then won a 63rd-minute penalty. At the other end, Shilton could not bear to look, turning his back and resting on his haunches, but Clarke dispatched the spot kick high into the corner of the net with Tomaszewski going the wrong way.

Currie tested Tomaszewski with a teasing cross that was perilously close to dropping underneath the bar before the keeper, who looked to have misread the flight of the ball, tipped it over. He also made a mess of an attempted punch clear, but somehow recovered to hack away Clarke's shot. In what was increasingly resembling a shooting gallery, Hunter was the next to be denied, Tomaszewski pushing the drive aside. Then he got his body behind Currie's strike to make another save. But Tomaszewski's best stop was a tremendous reaction save, turning the ball around the post from Clarke's close-range effort as England appealed in vain for another penalty after Bell had been sent sprawling by an apparent push. McFarland, England's last defender, was booked for blatantly pulling back the goal-bound Lato, an offence that in the modern game would be punished with a red card. Shilton also had to save at the feet of the lively Lato when the Polish raider did get through the England rearguard as the home side began to look ragged.

Try as they might, a tired, anguished England could not land a knockout blow, despite two frantic late scrambles. With Tomaszewski hopelessly out of position and almost fisting the ball into his own goal, substitute Kevin Hector – making his England debut after coming on for Chivers moments earlier – got on the end of Currie's left-wing corner, but saw his header cleared off the line before Channon knocked the loose ball agonisingly wide at the far post. It was as if there was a supernatural force field around the Poland goal as Tomaszewski then punched a high ball clear and managed to lay a foot on Bell's follow-up shot, but still needed a goal-line block by Mirosław Bulzacki to complete yet another Houdini-like escape. The final shot count was given as England 36, Poland two. But all that mattered was the scoreline: England 1 Poland 1.

The fact that the Poles had weathered such a welter of pressure remained a source of astonishment to the watching world. But what Clough and others had overlooked was that Kazimierz Górski's side, who had won Olympic gold in Munich in 1972, were a more than capable unit and proved as much by returning to the scene of that triumph to finish third at the World Cup with a victory over Brazil through Lato's solo strike. After they had confounded England, Geoffrey

Green, the august football correspondent of *The Times*, wrote prophetically of Poland, 'The fact that they survived such an onslaught and at the same time in passing moments showed their basic skills suggests that they may still have much to say for themselves in West Germany next summer.'

Ramsey's long, lonely, post-match walk around the perimeter of the pitch towards the Wembley tunnel served as a metaphor for the growing isolation he was feeling as England manager. Afterwards, he told the BBC's John Motson he was disappointed, 'Not for myself, particularly, but most certainly for the players because no one could have asked more from them. They played as well as they could possibly play and put everything they had into the game. If there was a failure, it was in the fact they couldn't score goals.'

Ramsey described Tomaszewski's performance as 'magnificent', and refused to single out Currie or Hunter for losing possession in the build-up to Poland's goal, only referring to them as 'an England player' and 'a defender' respectively. Ramsey was then pressed about his future, saying, 'What about it? I'm the England manager, aren't I? Like yourself, I've got to work to live.' Did he want to carry on doing the job? 'That's a leading question,' he said. 'Shall we wait and see?'

* * *

England's World Cup exit was a cataclysmic event for the national game and it came in what had already been a turbulent week as Brian Clough hogged the headlines with not only his words but his deeds. Only two days before England faced Poland, Clough and his assistant, Peter Taylor, had quit Derby County. Chairman Sam Longson, with whom Clough had repeatedly clashed, accepted their resignations and Rams fans were quick to launch protests, marching through the streets of the town and demanding the reinstatement of the managerial duo, who had taken Derby from Second Division title winners in 1969 to their first league championship three years later.

Clough stoked the mood by turning up as a spectator at a Derby home match and making sure the whole world could see him sitting in the stand. Even the Derby players submitted a letter to Longson calling for Clough and Taylor to be reappointed. One of Longson's big gripes was the amount of time Clough spent spouting his outspoken views on TV as a pundit. As the coverage of the Poland game proved, Longson's complaints were never going to make Clough change his ways. In the end, though, there was to be no messianic resurrection for 'Old Big 'Ead' at the Baseball Ground.

The following month, when Clough surprised everyone by taking charge of Third Division Brighton & Hove Albion, England were back at Wembley for their second friendly against Italy in exactly five months. Moore, captaining England for the 90th time and thereby equalling the record of Billy Wright, returned in place of a shattered Hunter, while Peter Osgood, who hadn't made an international appearance since coming on as a substitute against Czechoslovakia at the 1970 World Cup, was also recalled at the expense of Chivers. But it would be the final time the two returnees would play for their country. Moore, who died tragically young at 51 on 24 February 1993 after a battle with cancer, made his 108th appearance in an England shirt and his last match, in particular, would signal a further step towards a new epoch. Capello proved himself the scourge of the English, scoring against them again when he knocked in a scruffy 86th-minute goal from close range after Shilton – in the Tunnel End goal where he conceded against Poland – had only tamely parried a low Giorgio Chinaglia cross from the right. It was the only goal of the game but Capello made an impression of a different sort in the first half when he committed a cynical challenge on Currie, who required treatment from England trainer Harold Shepherdson. But the Italians were almost punished when the resulting free kick was worked to an indignant Currie, who unleashed a fierce drive that crashed into the side netting at keeper Dino Zoff's near upright. It was an all-action Currie and he managed to get another shot on goal despite slipping on the greasy surface, but Zoff had his near post covered and made a razor-sharp save. Bell was unlucky not to score when he fired across goal, where Italy skipper Giacinto Facchetti was fortunate not to divert the ball into his own net. Currie continued to worry the *Azzurri*, pulling a shot wide with Zoff extended. The lethal Luigi Riva provided Shilton with some work, and a good save was needed to keep the score goalless, but Zoff had to be on his toes to tip over a piledriver by Hughes, who then thumped another effort from distance narrowly wide.

In many ways, though, it was a typical display from Italy, and as the game wore on there was a growing feeling that they were reeling their opponents in for the sucker punch – which was duly delivered. Defeat was a fitting finish to a calendar year that had ultimately proved an *annus horribilis* for England. At the end of the game, Italian fans clambered over pitchside partitions to celebrate their side's maiden victory on English soil.

Officially, Ramsey still had the support of the FA, but Sir Harold Thompson, destined to become chairman and whose relationship with the manager had always been tense to say the least, was one in the corridors of power turning up the heat behind the scenes. Ramsey ignited more intrigue when he presented the FA with proposals aimed at boosting England's future prospects. In doing so, he raised the eternal 'club versus country' debate. One of his key suggestions was for there to be an international match on a much more regular basis, perhaps as often as each month. In practice, however, the idea was unworkable and he was left in no doubt about what he was up against when club managers refused to release players for England's friendly in Portugal, which came towards the climax of the domestic season and was viewed by some as largely meaningless against the background of failure to qualify for the World Cup. It underlined an essential problem – ultimately, Ramsey had little control over the availability of players.

Treating the then-annual Football League v Scottish League fixture as a de facto England-Scotland game had been one way of scrutinising established international players and those on the fringes. For instance, in March 1970, three months before the start of the World Cup, Ramsey was in charge of the Football League XI against their Scottish counterparts in a 3-2 victory at Coventry City's Highfield Road. With both eyes clearly fixed on that summer's tournament, Ramsey fielded a Football League line-up consisting of four players – Peters, Hughes, goalkeeper Alex Stepney and striker Jeff Astle – who would help to make up the 22-man squad he finally settled on for Mexico. But the side also included three players in World Cup contention: midfielder Ralph Coates and striker Brian Kidd would make the provisional party of 28 before being omitted, and midfielder Colin Harvey, who was named among the additional 12 reserves in the initial pool of 40. Also in action against the Scottish League were McFarland and fellow defender Colin Todd, who would become Derby team-mates a year later when the latter moved from Sunderland and were both destined to become England players.

To underscore the store that was placed on the inter-league matches, the likes of Moore and Geoff Hurst also featured in the March 1971 clash, in which the English were 1-0 winners at Hampden Park with a goal by Coates.

Both Moore and Hurst were also in the Football League side that won 3-2 at Middlesbrough's Ayresome Park in March 1972, when Currie struck twice and defender Mike Doyle scored. In fact, Moore was still involved 12 months later when the Football League were held to a 2-2 draw at Hampden, where Channon bagged a brace. Other England regulars who figured for the Football League side in the early to mid-1970s included Shilton and goalkeeping rival Ray Clemence, Storey and Bell. Dwindling interest and attendances, however, would soon see the Football League-Scottish League encounters, which had begun as far back as the early 1890s, peter out.

A similar fate befell other representative matches involving the Football League, who in September 1971 were 2-1 winners over the League of Ireland at Lansdowne Road, Dublin, where the visitors were captained by England keeper Banks in a side ladened with fellow internationals. Two of them, Arsenal's John Radford and Chelsea's Osgood, with a penalty, were the Football League's scorers.

In pressing the case for the prioritisation of the England side in the wake of the shattering World Cup calamity, it was evident that Ramsey was giving vent to his frustrations. Yet there can be no question he was literally ahead of the game. Over time, world football's governing body, FIFA, would toughen their regulations and make it obligatory for clubs to release players to their countries.

Of course, a shift in the balance of power on that score was never going to arrive soon enough to ease Ramsey's plight. It was a little rich that one of the club managers who had kept his players at home was Ramsey's successor-in-waiting: Leeds boss Don Revie. A three-game losing run – threatening his side's ultimate First Division title triumph that season – in the lead-up to England's match in Portugal was manifestly a material consideration in Revie's thinking.

Whatever his attitude was at that point towards the low ebb surrounding England, it paid off for Revie as Leeds recorded a 2-0 home win against Derby three days after Ramsey's revamped team had drawn a blank.

The cluttered nature of the football calendar meant that Ramsey was also hit hard by Liverpool manager Bill Shankly, understandably, holding on to players for the FA Cup semi-final replay with Leicester City, which was staged at Villa Park on the same night as England's game and won 3-1 by the Reds on their way to beating Newcastle in that year's final. An inspired Kevin Keegan scored one against Leicester, who had Shilton in goal, and Hughes skippered Liverpool. All three were in the England team when they faced Wales under a month later.

As for Ramsey, in the slipstream of the defeat by Italy, the overarching impression was that time was running out on his tenure. He had been left clinging to his job for five more months before the visit to Lisbon's Estádio da Luz on 3 April 1974. Six new caps were dished out to Queens Park Rangers goalkeeper Phil Parkes, Stoke left-back Mike Pejic, Sunderland centre-back Dave Watson, Burnley midfielder Martin Dobson, West Ham midfielder Trevor Brooking and QPR forward Stan Bowles. For all his dissatisfaction, Ramsey had made use of an opportunity to assess the credentials of some new faces.

But the goalless draw with Portugal was memorable for only one thing: it was Ramsey's last match as England manager. On 2 May, in a typically stuffy statement, the FA announced that Ramsey had been relieved of his duties. The statement read, 'The committees of the FA, which have been considering the future of English football, have examined some aspects in detail and progress has been made. Following the meetings, a unanimous recommendation was submitted to the executive committee that Sir Alf Ramsey should be replaced as England team manager.' The statement went on to confirm that Joe Mercer, then general manager at Coventry, had agreed to take over but 'does not wish to be considered for the job as permanent manager'. It was left to FA secretary Ted Croker to elaborate a little and bring a touch of warmth and humanity in responding to the end of Ramsey's reign. He said, 'There was a termination clause in his contract. At no time was he asked to resign.' Croker added, 'All I would like to say is that I feel sadness that this sort of thing happens. Sir Alf has achieved tremendous things in everything he has tackled. A man of both his ability and integrity is not easy to find.'

Ramsey's critics could not argue with his record of 69 wins and only 17 defeats in 113 games in charge. Above all else, though, his 'Wingless Wonders' had been World Cup winners. Sadly, football is a capricious business and, to the game's eternal shame – particularly those at the FA at the time – Ramsey was largely shunned after losing the England job, for which it was said he was paid a relatively paltry £7,000 a year. In February 1970, he had turned down the opportunity to manage Portuguese aristocrats Benfica. Ramsey's explanation for his decision spoke volumes about his sense of patriotism and loyalty. He said, 'I shall not go abroad. I'm an Englishman and English football is my life.'

There was a short spell in charge of struggling Birmingham City in the 1977/78 season, when he replaced Willie Bell. Ramsey steered the Blues away from danger, though he was unable to complete the season due to poor health. Then came a brief stint as technical director with Greek giants Panathinaikos, before retirement in 1980. Alzheimer's affected Ramsey in later life and he died aged 79 on 28 April 1999.

5

Backroom Boys

AT THE highest level of the game in the 21st century, 'backroom' staff are a team themselves, often numbering as many as those they are responsible for on the pitch. Yet when England won the World Cup in 1966, ostensibly there were only two key men who assisted Alf Ramsey on the football front – Harold Shepherdson and Les Cocker. Shepherdson was Ramsey's right-hand man for the entirety of his 11 and a half years as England manager. His association with England, however, lasted longer than Ramsey's. In fact, at least in terms of front-line football staff, it lasted longer than anyone else in the history of the national team – a staggering 17 years.

Shepherdson was 'trainer' at hometown club Middlesbrough when Walter Winterbottom invited him to work with England in 1957, a year before the World Cup finals in Sweden. That tournament was the first of four that 'Shep' was involved in, with the glory of 1966 sandwiched between Chile in 1962 and Mexico in 1970. He even stayed on as assistant to caretaker manager Joe Mercer when Ramsey was dismissed in 1974. The lighter side to Shepherdson's nature, in contrast to the stiff formality of Ramsey, went down well with players. In 1993, he showed that his sense of humour had endured when it was mistakenly reported that he was dead. Like Mark Twain, Shepherdson said that reports of his death had been 'greatly exaggerated'. Middlesbrough-born Don Revie's appointment as Ramsey's permanent replacement brought about an end to Shepherdson's time with England.

Awarded an MBE in 1969 and, posthumously, a World Cup winners' medal in 2009, Shepherdson remained a servant of Middlesbrough, where his curtailed playing career as a centre-half had begun as an amateur in 1932. World War Two, in which he held the rank of staff sergeant as an army physical training instructor, intervened and, on the resumption of his playing days, he found his first-team opportunities limited with Boro and joined Southend United where his career was cut short in 1947 by a knee injury.

Boro, then managed by Bolton and Arsenal legend and former England inside-forward David Jack, re-employed him as a trainer and he went on to work under a string of bosses at Ayresome Park, as well as stepping in as caretaker manager on four occasions, when Raich Carter (1966), Stan Anderson (1973), Jack Charlton (1977) and Bobby Murdoch (1982) left their jobs, before he finally retired from an active role with the Teessiders as chief executive (football) in 1983. Shepherdson died on 13 September 1995, aged 76.

David Mills played under Shepherdson, whose son-in-law, left-back Frank Spraggon, was the forward's team-mate at Middlesbrough. Mills, who scored three goals in his eight appearances for the England under-23 side between 1973 and 1976, recalled, 'When I joined Boro in the late 1960s, Harold was effectively assistant manager to Stan Anderson, who was player-manager. Stan was relatively young because he was still playing, so Harold did a lot of the off-field stuff. He was very experienced at that level and he was the sort of father figure at the club. For instance, he was the one who, after the scouts had initially seen me play, sort of took over and liaised with my father about me signing as an apprentice. He looked after the admin side and youth development to a degree. He would talk to us as young players in a sort of pastoral role.

'Harold was very much a behind-the-scenes operator. He was also somebody who knew the club and everybody around Middlesbrough ... all the scouts and the people they employed. He was a bit of an institution, I suppose, with the number of years he spent at the club. He was with Middlesbrough longer than he was with England – and he was with England a long time. Harold was the archetypal trainer, the old sponge man. The only time I saw him on the training pitch was when he was caretaker manager. He was a very friendly, affable guy and he was immaculate as well. I can't really remember seeing him without a collar and tie on apart from his time on the training pitch. And I'm surprised he didn't wear one then!

'From a football point of view, as first-team players we didn't have a lot to do with him. The only time was when he took over as caretaker manager for the second half of the 1972/73 season after Stan departed. I remember we played Blackpool at home and I was having a poor game to put it mildly – and the crowd were quite vociferous in confirming that. They were slaughtering me and it was one of those situations where the more you tried, the more you got involved, the worse it was getting. I was always in the thick of things, but I was always making mistakes. It went on and on and on ... but we beat them 2-0 and I scored both goals!

'And after the second goal, I went to the Holgate End and I stuck two fingers up with both hands. Of course, the crowd reaction got worse in terms of the abuse. There was no fence, just a little wall, and I thought they were going to come over the wall and come after me. At the end of the game, we came off the pitch and I was waiting for the consequences from Harold as caretaker manager. And what he said to me went something like this: "You've made it really hard for yourself now," he said. "It will take you a while to win them back over. I understand your frustration and I understand what you did and why you did it. In fact, to be honest, if it had been me, I think I would have pulled my shorts down and shown them my backside." That wasn't what I was expecting! It certainly took the tension out of the situation, that's for sure. I wasn't fined, I didn't get chucked out of the team. I just carried on as though nothing had happened. I think Harold knew that it was going to be a test of character for me to get through the following months – and eventually I did.'

The following season, the 1973/74 campaign, Shepherdson was alongside Jack Charlton, Anderson's permanent successor, when Mills scored the goal that clinched Middlesbrough's promotion to the old First Division as Second Division champions. Mills said, 'When Jack came in as manager, Harold continued in a similar role. Jack knew him from their time together with England and 1966 in particular.'

As well as Shepherdson, another England figure was instrumental in Charlton becoming Middlesbrough manager: Dr Neil Phillips. The Welshman, who moved to the north-east to take up a general practitioner's position in Redcar, became Middlesbrough's club doctor and was elevated to vice-chairman. Through his Ayresome Park links with Shepherdson, 'Doc' Phillips was introduced to the inner sanctum of Ramsey's England regime. After being appointed as the under-23 team doctor, Phillips was promoted to duty with the senior side in a twist of fate shortly before the 1966 World Cup. Alan Bass was England's senior doctor, but had used up his holiday entitlement and was unable to join Ramsey's squad at Lilleshall as they prepared for the tournament. Bass did return to the fold for England's World Cup triumph and was sitting next to Ramsey on the bench during the final, but Phillips remained part of the medical team. Four years later, Phillips was England's doctor at the World Cup in Mexico, where he had to face the acute crisis of goalkeeper Gordon Banks being laid low with a stomach upset and missing the 3-2 quarter-final defeat by West Germany. Phillips, who died on 21 March 2015, aged 83, served with the FA until Ramsey's departure in 1974.

Mills remembers Phillips as more influential than many would have imagined. He said, 'He was viewed highly from a medical point of view, but he got involved a bit on the football side of things while he was at Middlesbrough. I remember having discussions with him contract-wise. He became a director and he was the sort of liaison between the board and the players, not necessarily in terms of negotiating contracts, but discussing the players' futures. I think, because he was a younger member of the board, they probably felt he was the best equipped to deal with younger people. It was unusual, I suppose, for a GP. He was very much a football enthusiast but, being Welsh, he was a rugby person as well. The connection between 1966, when Harold and Neil Phillips were both involved with England and Jack as a player, I think that had a significant influence when they decided to offer Jack the job. I think the bottom line was, from what I could gather, Jack had seen us play prior to taking the job and had been significantly impressed. I don't think he would have taken the job if he'd felt the group of players he was inheriting weren't up to the job that he was hoping to do. Jack had just finished playing and I'm sure he wasn't short of other offers because of his pedigree. But I'm also sure that Neil and Harold were influential in persuading Jack that the right thing to do was to come to Middlesbrough. Had they not been involved, he may well have made a different choice, I don't know.'

Both Shepherdson and Phillips had also prevailed in the decision of Charlton's World Cup-winning colleague Nobby Stiles to move to Teesside from Manchester United.

The midfielder, whose final game for England had been a year earlier, joined Boro in 1971 and stayed for two seasons, making 69 appearances in league and cup, but Charlton was happy to let him move on. As it turned out, Stiles swapped one Charlton brother for another, joining former Old Trafford team-mate Bobby, who had taken charge of Preston North End, and becoming player-coach at Deepdale.

Mills said, 'Nobby got the opportunity to go back closer to home. I think there was maybe a bit of a conflict of personalities as well between Nobby and Jack, which you could probably trace back to their England days, because they were both strong characters. You could imagine them not necessarily agreeing all the time on everything. Being the strong personalities they were, they would be quite stubborn the pair of them, I would think.' But Mills insists Stiles had something of a double persona, saying, 'Nobby was top-drawer. He was arguably the nicest person I've ever met in football. You would never imagine that if you looked at him on the field. He had this split personality. He became a completely different person on the field. Off the field, he was an absolute gem.'

Mills, who credits Charlton with making him a better player, also remembers his manager's quirks. He said, 'Where do you start with Jack? He was a players' manager. I think he helped to develop me and improve me as a player. I played under him twice, at Boro and Sheffield Wednesday. When he took me to Sheff Wed, I lived with him and his wife, Pat, at their house in Barnsley. I came back from training one day and there was a note on the door saying, "We've gone to the shops, if we're not back by five o'clock, can you feed the hens?" He was a character.'

As a centre-back with Leeds, Charlton was also closely connected with Cocker. Born in Stockport, Cocker started off as a striker with his hometown club before moving to

Accrington Stanley. He was a coach at Luton Town and in 1960 joined Leeds, where he began to forge his famous alliance with Revie, who the following year was appointed player-manager in succession to Jack Taylor.

Having worked with Ramsey and Shepherdson at the World Cups of 1966 and 1970, and been Revie's long-time number two at Leeds, it was no surprise when Cocker followed him to be promoted in the England setup and continue as his assistant. As it was with Shepherdson, it was Winterbottom who introduced Cocker to the international scene in 1962. His reputation had grown and he was among the first to receive coaching badges at Lilleshall, where the FA established their School of Excellence. Like Shepherdson again, in 2009 Cocker was awarded a medal for his part in England's finest moment in 1966, but did not live to receive it, having died aged only 55 on 4 October 1979. Two years earlier, he had gone to the United Arab Emirates as Revie's assistant and had only been back in England for a short time, coaching under former Leeds captain Billy Bremner at Doncaster Rovers, when he passed away.

Cocker made clear his devotion to Revie during his time with England, saying, 'I will stay in Don Revie's shadow. There're a lot of people who would give anything to be in the same position. What have I got to achieve by leaving him unless there's a better job that is offered? I don't think I can find a better job than under him. Oh yes, I've had offers. When Don left to take the England job and before he asked me to join him, a First Division and Second Division club came in for me. I wasn't interested.' Cocker's loyalty to Revie was also evident in 1973 when Everton were interested in luring the manager away from Leeds. Revie urged Cocker to talk to his wife about the possibility of him joining the Toffees as his assistant. 'I told him "yes", said Cocker. 'I knew the wife would understand without asking her.'

Scotsman Bill Taylor was also on Revie's backroom staff with England as a trainer. Taylor worked under Alec Stock at Fulham when, with former England captains Bobby Moore and Alan Mullery in their side, the Craven Cottage outfit reached the 1975 FA Cup Final, losing 2-0 to West Ham. Ron Greenwood was by then the general manager of the Hammers, having handed over first-team responsibilities to John Lyall. When Greenwood became England manager after Revie's resignation in 1977, he appointed Taylor – by then coaching at Manchester City – as chief coach and recruited 1966 hero Geoff Hurst, who was in charge of non-league Telford and had, of course, played under Greenwood at West Ham. Taylor, who went on to coach at Oldham Athletic, had been a midfielder with Leyton Orient, Nottingham Forest and Lincoln City. He died tragically young, aged just 42, with a brain tumour on 30 November 1981, while still with England and little more than six months before Greenwood led his side to the World Cup in Spain.

Fred Street became a familiar face on the touchline for England. A long-time servant of his local club, Arsenal, he was a physio who was much more in the modern-day mould. Street started as a physio in football at Stoke City under Tony Waddington before a lengthy association with Arsenal's 1971 double-winning manager Bertie Mee led to him moving to Highbury. It was Revie who introduced Street to the England setup in 1974 and he also served under Greenwood, Bobby Robson and Graham Taylor in his 20 years with the FA, including three World Cup tournaments in 1982, 1986 and 1990. Dr Vernon Edwards was another long-serving member of England's medical staff, joining the FA under Ramsey and later becoming senior team doctor until 1986 when he stepped down on health grounds during Robson's reign after suffering a heart attack at the World Cup in Mexico in the summer of that year.

Almost four decades later, football has a whole new generation of backroom boys, with the introduction of technology and sports science personnel informing performance, tactics, fitness and treatment of injuries. The game has come a long way since the days of the old 'magic sponge'.

6

Uncle Joe

SIR ALF Ramsey's dismissal as England manager came a mere month before the British Home Championship, meaning the FA had needed to act to install a replacement. For the first time in their history, they opted to bring in a caretaker boss and chose Joe Mercer, one of the most experienced and popular men in football.

Due to a packed May-June schedule consisting of seven matches, he would be in the England hot seat for more games than future caretaker managers Howard Wilkinson, Stuart Pearce and Peter Taylor combined. As a player, he had represented Everton and Arsenal and would have surely won more than his five caps had it not been for the outbreak of World War Two. Along with the likes of Walter Winterbottom, he helped in the war effort by drilling army recruits. He went on to manage Sheffield United and Aston Villa following his retirement from playing, but it was at Manchester City where he would achieve legendary status. The First Division title, FA Cup, Football League Cup, European Cup Winners' Cup and the Charity Shield were all won by Mercer during a remarkable six-year spell as manager. He was in the midst of winding down his career with Coventry City when the FA came calling. His sense of humour was infectious. Allegedly, when the FA's receptionist asked if he had an appointment, he replied, 'Yes, for seven matches.'

In his autobiography *Crazy Horse*, the title of which referred to his nickname, Emlyn Hughes said of Mercer, 'Joe came breezing in and everything was done for a laugh. Whereas Sir Alf had done everything correctly and straight down the line, Joe had little time for formalities. He was just what the team needed at this particular time.' Mercer opted for Hughes as one of his temporary right-hand men in the days before inflated coaching teams, giving the defender the privilege of wearing the captain's armband in all of his matches in charge, as well as frequently asking him for his advice on player selection. Behind Mercer's jovial demeanour, however, there was pain that was well hidden by his smile. He had become very unwell during his time at Villa, suffering a stroke in the mid-1960s, and his playing career had been beset by serious injuries, most notably a broken leg in 1954. By the time he took the reins with England, he was also suffering from excruciating back pain. It could be said that he had given his body and soul to football, and in 1974 his dedication was rewarded with an opportunity to take the biggest job in the English game.

Wales provided his first opposition at Ninian Park on 11 May 1974 in the opener of that year's Home Championship. With Leighton James and Terry Yorath among their number, the Welsh were a fair side, yet the fact that they had not scored against England in the competition for four years said much about the limitations of their attack. Mercer awarded a maiden cap to Keith Weller of Leicester City, while Stan Bowles was given another chance to impress. The game was rather open in the early exchanges until Weller hammered a cross-cum-shot at keeper John Phillips, who could only paw the ball towards the feet of the grateful Bowles to tap home.

The next goal settled the game, Kevin Keegan scoring his first at international level in comical fashion with his tame volley creeping over the line after Tony Villars made a hash of an attempted clearance. Peter Shilton was later required to tip the ball over the bar from a shot by John Mahoney, but ultimately Mercer achieved a straightforward win in his first game at the helm.

Evidently sufficiently impressed, he fielded an unchanged line-up against Northern Ireland four days later. England toiled against a good side, Weller eventually breaking the deadlock in the second half. This match-winning goal was created by Weller's Leicester team-mate Frank Worthington, who was making his debut from the bench.

Scotland had won one of their two fixtures going into their showdown with England at Hampden Park. As it stood, England needed just a draw to lift the trophy, while a Scotland win would mean it would be shared due to goal difference not being factored into the final table. An injury to Roy McFarland in the previous game led to a return to the defence for Norman Hunter. Another member of Mercer's squad was unavailable. Bowles, never a stranger to controversy, had a heated exchange with the manager over his decision to substitute him for Worthington against Northern Ireland, and the Queens Park Rangers man subsequently walked out on the squad.

The match would be Mercer's lowest moment as caretaker manager, though it may have turned out even worse if Shilton had not been in impressive form. In just the fourth minute, left-back Mike Pejic, in his fourth and final England appearance, deflected a Joe Jordan shot into the net. Worthington then had an opportunity to level the scores after Jim Holton inadvertently headed the ball on for him, but his volley went just over the bar. There was little Shilton could do to prevent Scotland's second; Kenny Dalglish crossed low into the box and for the second time that afternoon an England player diverted the ball into his own net, Colin Todd the unfortunate player in this instance. A consolation was almost salvaged with a header from none other than Martin Peters. Playing his last game for England, he was the only member of the World Cup-winning side in Mercer's line-up that day, and it was a pity that his illustrious international career would end with a defeat. Scotland, however, were deserved winners, and for the first time serious questions were being asked of the new-look England. The Home Championship was therefore left tied, an outcome that satisfied no one, not least the Scottish who had finished with a marginally superior goal difference to England.

On 22 May, England faced Argentina at Wembley in a friendly. Though the rivalry between the two nations was not quite as intense as it would later become, few in England had forgotten their ugly encounter in the 1966 World Cup in which disruptive Argentina captain Antonio Rattín was sent off and Ramsey later branded the opposition 'animals'. Unusually, an Argentinian official was chosen to referee the friendly at the behest of the away side, who still blamed the officiating for their loss eight years earlier. David Nish, as well as fellow full-back Pejic, had played his last game for his country, and Dave Watson and debutant Alec Lindsay replaced them. Leading the attack once more were Mick Channon and Worthington, two of the most dangerous English players of the decade. It was the former who scored the opening goal of the game when Colin Bell fed him a through ball, Channon coolly rounding keeper Daniel Carnevali to add to his international tally. The Southampton striker was unfortunate not to have scored earlier in the match when Carnevali produced a wonderful save in turning his effort against the bar.

In the 54th minute, Bell struck the upright allowing Worthington to showcase his own ability, the forward scoring with a clever flick with his back to the Argentinian goal. A rare misjudgement from Shilton gave Argentina a route back into the game when he came out for a cross which he should have left for his defence to clear, and Mario Kempes knocked the ball into an empty net. Galvanised by the goal, Argentina began to look increasingly threatening. The home fans were on tenterhooks when Hughes gave away a penalty for a clumsy challenge on Kempes in the last minute of regular time. Kempes would dispatch the penalty with aplomb to earn his side a 2-2 draw. Boos rang out at the final whistle, the referee the target of the crowd's disgust. Under different circumstances, this result could have been creditable as England were up against an adept team, but the home side had thrown away a two-goal lead in the worst way imaginable. On a wound-up Hughes becoming involved in an altercation at half-time with Argentinian players, Mercer commented, 'I told him he was out of order. His pride was hurt and he got himself involved. It was his own fault. This was the very thing I had warned players about before the game.'

England had little time to regroup. Following the Argentina match, the FA had arranged a tour of eastern Europe, an interesting choice of destination given that the Cold War was then at its midway point. Their first stop of the tour was Leipzig, East Germany. For most of the travelling party, the experience would be an unpleasant one. In *Crazy Horse*, Hughes said, 'Most of us hardly saw outside of our hotels, apart from training and playing. Bulgaria was probably the worst. The hotel was poor and the moment anyone stepped out of the front door he was mobbed by people asking for ball-point pens or money.' It is worth stressing that most of the squad had rarely played outside western Europe for either club or country, so visiting poverty-ridden nations like those under the control of communism must have come as a serious culture shock to them.

Having qualified for the 1974 World Cup, East Germany were using the England friendly as preparation for the tournament. As a team, they were stubborn and well organised, and these traits were very much on display at the World Cup, during which they achieved their most famous victory, a 1-0 win over uneasy neighbours West Germany. There was a recall for Martin Dobson to the England team. Remarkably, the Burnley midfielder would end his international career having played under three different managers despite only winning five caps in total. England played out a frustrating 1-1 draw. Having hit the woodwork on several occasions, their inefficacy was punished when Joachim Streich – who would later become both his nation's leading scorer and record cap holder – expertly controlled the ball in the box and scored with a brilliant, curling shot. Fortunately for England, it took barely over a minute for parity to be restored. They were awarded a free kick 20 yards out in a central position from which Channon found the net with a low effort. Mercer did not turn to his substitutes for inspiration despite the scoreline.

On 1 June, England faced Bulgaria in Sofia. Even though they had played in a different country only three days before, an unchanged side was named. Worthington scored the only goal of the game in what was a routine win. Though their success against the Bulgarians had been generally uneventful, their arrival at the next stop of the tour was anything but. There are contradictory accounts of how the incident at Belgrade airport began, with Lindsay clambering on to a luggage carousel either as a joke or to dislodge his bag which had become entangled. Whatever it was that initially caught the eye of the Yugoslavian security guards, their reaction was entirely unwarranted. Firstly, Lindsay was grabbed by the security staff and held against a wall. Having witnessed his team-mate being accosted, Keegan's initial reaction was to begin laughing at the farcical situation that had unfolded in front of him, but the guards, presumably, considered his obvious amusement to be a show of insolence. Keegan, his bags containing pottery which he had bought in Bulgaria for his family, was lifted from the ground. In his autobiography *My Life in Football*, he said of the incident, 'Everything happened so quickly, I wondered at first if it was one of the other lads messing around, but the sheer amount of force made me realise it was sinister. My carrier bag split open and the pottery smashed on the floor. I swung my arm back instinctively to try to fend off whoever it was. Then a guy in uniform appeared and suddenly there were two of them on me. This one was a policeman, and when I was dragged into a side room, the battering really began.'

After being subjected to a prolonged beating, Keegan was forced to his knees and kept in the position for 20 minutes. Thankfully, FA secretary Ted Croker arrived and explained that the man who they had assaulted was in fact one of the biggest sports stars on the continent. The police attempted to clean the blood from his face and clothing, but the beating they had delivered had been so severe that it was a futile task trying to hide what they had done. So incensed were the other players when they caught sight of their battered team-mate that there were rumblings from some of departing from the country at the soonest opportunity. Mercer talked them round, though Keegan himself was not among those that needed convincing.

So, on 5 June, they took to the field in Belgrade. For the first time since 1966, an unchanged England team was named for the third successive game. The match started well for the visitors. Just six minutes in, keeper Enver Marić flapped at a Keegan corner and the ball landed at the feet of Trevor Brooking. The midfielder's shot was initially kept out, but Marić fell over as he began desperately backpedalling, and Channon picked up the rebound to finish. The lead did not last long. Bell was not quite able to latch on to a headed clearance from Watson and Ilija Petković launched an attack with a simple pass. Having been fed the ball, Ivica Šurjak dinked a cross for the onrushing Petković to head home. Disaster almost struck early after the restart when Watson nearly diverted a cross into his own net. As it happened, Ray Clemence soon conceded his second of the night. Branko Oblak, who would go on to play for Bayern Munich three years later, scored an absolute howitzer that was such a powerful strike that the England keeper barely reacted. It had been a goal worthy of winning any match, yet there was one player on the pitch more determined than any to leave their mark on the game.

Still sporting several bruises, it is fair to say Keegan had a score to settle. Lindsay cropped up in an advanced position and flicked the ball in the direction of the six-yard box and, after a Yugoslavian foot had inadvertently knocked the ball towards him, Keegan bravely dived forward to beat Marić. The Liverpool forward insisted after the game that he would never again play in the country, a vow which became a serious issue years later when he was with Hamburg and the German side drew Hajduk Spilt in the European Cup. England had a late chance for a winner when Malcolm Macdonald found himself through on goal after a surging run, yet his shot went narrowly wide. The match ended 2-2, meaning England had finished their tour undefeated. The referee's whistle would also signal an end to Mercer's tenure.

After the game, Mercer was asked by ITV's Hugh Johns if he would be prepared to stay on as England's manager. 'With all the sciatica I've got? A 60-year-old manager with sciatica; it doesn't make much sense, does it?' he playfully replied before quickly turning attention back to the team. In the same interview, he spoke of how he was aware that England did not possess the technical abilities of the Brazilians, but that he believed there was more to the game than just flair, such as 'heart, courage and organisation and belief … belief in England. I believe in England.' Mercer had done much more than simply keep the hot seat warm; he had brought confidence back to the team as well as softening the blow of Ramsey's departure. The FA were impressed by Mercer and there were even rumours that they were considering offering him the role permanently. In truth, even if he had won all seven of his games in charge, the job had already shown signs that it was taking a toll on him, and Mercer would have surely turned down the position if he had been offered it full-time. He had picked up the blueprint that Ramsey had mapped out in the belief that the players he had picked would be integral to England's future. As it turned out, Don Revie had very different views on how to take the team forward. One of the most unusual aspects of 1974 in relation to the England team was how the careers of some players both started and ended that year. Worthington, Weller, Pejic, Lindsay, Dobson and keeper Phil Parkes gathered all their caps in 1974. By the winter, these players, who had been earmarked by Ramsey, would be discarded and the new manager would transform the selection policy dramatically.

Results under Mercer were less than stellar, but he deserves much credit for navigating England through a series of difficult friendlies. Colin Bell, who had played hundreds of games under him at Manchester City, praised Mercer in his autobiography, *Colin Bell, Reluctant Hero*, saying, 'Joe knew he was only a stop-gap manager, which took all the pressure off him and the players … we did really well at that time and played the sort of football I enjoyed based on passing and movement and, most of all, attacking.' Mercer would never manage a first-team match again, becoming a director at Coventry in 1975, then retiring from the game altogether six years later. He died on his 76th birthday, 9 August 1990. His time as caretaker manager of England could be viewed as a period of quiet before a storm. What would follow him would be a tumultuous phase for the national team.

7

Famine and the Feast

ENGLISH FOOTBALL had something of a split personality in the 1970s. While the international side were floundering, the nation's leading clubs were proudly flying the flag in Europe. Liverpool emerged as the dominant force both at home and abroad, but others gatecrashed the party. The incomparable Bill Shankly transformed the Anfield outfit in the 1960s, but after his surprise retirement in 1974, having just won the FA Cup for the second time and a year earlier having led the Reds to a third Football League title under his tutelage and eighth in their history, it was loyal right-hand man Bob Paisley who succeeded him to build on the legacy of the garrulous Scot. Shankly was the first Liverpool manager to win a European trophy, the UEFA Cup in 1973. It was the platform for them to eventually become the most decorated British club in European competition.

The modest Paisley hailed from Hetton-le-Hole in County Durham and was a former Liverpool left-half who made more than 250 league appearances for the club. He added three further First Division championships – in the space of four seasons – to take their '70s collection to four. The crowning glories were European Cup Final victories in 1977 and 1978.

* * *

In the 1970s, English clubs won 12 major European trophies – one in early 1980 owing to extenuating circumstances. That haul comprised three European Cups, two European Cup Winners' Cups, three UEFA Cups, two Inter-Cities Fairs Cups, and two European Super Cups. Brian Clough's Nottingham Forest emulated Liverpool by winning two successive European Cups, the first in 1979.

Having picked up one UEFA Cup, a second soon came Liverpool's way in 1976, but Tottenham Hotspur had already beaten them to it by winning the inaugural competition in 1972. It was an all-English final as they defeated Wolverhampton Wanderers over two legs. The first at Molineux was refereed by Tofiq Bahramov, the Soviet Union linesman who awarded Geoff Hurst's controversial second goal in the 1966 World Cup Final. England striker Martin Chivers scored twice for Spurs while Jim McCalliog – scorer of Scotland's winner when Sir Alf Ramsey's side suffered their first defeat as world champions – netted as Wolves lost 2-1. The second leg at White Hart Lane was a 1-1 draw, with England midfielder and Spurs skipper Alan Mullery scoring for the home side as they secured an aggregate triumph. The UEFA Cup had replaced the Inter-Cities Fairs Cup, which was won by Arsenal in 1970 and Leeds United in 1971, also in two-legged finals. Spurs were beaten in the final of the UEFA Cup in 1974 when they lost 4-2 on aggregate to Feyenoord. The first leg in north London was drawn 2-2, but the Dutch side won the return 2-0 on a night of shame for Spurs as their fans rioted in Rotterdam. Chivers and fellow England internationals Martin Peters and Ralph Coates played in both games.

In the Cup Winners' Cup, Manchester City were winners in 1970 after beating Polish side Górnik Zabrze 2-1 in Vienna. Górnik included Włodzimierz Lubański, Jerzy

Gorgoń and Jan Banaś, who would all figure for Poland in the destruction of England's bid to reach the 1974 World Cup. But Joe Mercer's City, with Francis Lee – bound for the World Cup with England in the summer of 1970 – converting a penalty, edged a 2-1 victory watched by only 7,968.

A year later, it was Chelsea celebrating in the Cup Winners' Cup and there was another all-English affair when they met City over two legs in the semi-finals where the Londoners won 1-0 both home and away. Chelsea then overcame Real Madrid in a Piraeus final which required a replay. England striker Peter Osgood struck in a 1-1 draw and grabbed the Blues' second goal in a 2-1 win second time around. The opposition were somewhat less formidable for the holders the following season in the first round in one of the quirkier European football stories as Chelsea beat Luxembourg's Jeunesse Hautcharage – who included a one-armed striker, a player wearing spectacles and four brothers – 21-0 on aggregate. In the second leg at Stamford Bridge, the Blues achieved a club-record 13-0 romp. Osgood, having scored a hat-trick in the first leg, bagged another five goals.

West Ham failed to match the success of their London rivals, losing 4-2 to Anderlecht in the 1976 Cup Winners' Cup Final. The Belgian giants had the advantage of playing on home soil at the Heysel Stadium in Brussels, but the Hammers took the lead through Pat Holland, courtesy of Trevor Brooking's delivery. Keith Robson then had to drag them back into the game after that advantage was squandered, but Holland gave away a penalty and West Ham were punished as they conceded twice inside the last 20 minutes of a pulsating match. It was a disappointment for the Hammers, who had won the competition in 1965 when Bobby Moore lifted the trophy after victory over Munich 1860 at Wembley, where a year later he performed similar duties for England.

Arsenal's climactic 3-2 FA Cup victory over Manchester United in the 'five-minute final' of 1979, when the Gunners threw away a 2-0 lead in the last five minutes only to snatch the silverware with Alan Sunderland's 89th-minute strike, set them on a Cup Winners' Cup trail which led, like West Ham, to a final in Brussels. It was there, in 1980, that Arsenal suffered a 5-4 defeat on penalties to Spanish side Valencia after the scoresheet remained blank following extra time.

Again over two legs, and then contested by the European Cup holders and Cup Winners' Cup winners, the European Super Cup was won by Liverpool in 1977 and Nottingham Forest two seasons later. The Merseysiders beat a Hamburg side, containing recently departed Kop idol Kevin Keegan, 6-0 in the second leg at Anfield after a 1-1 draw in West Germany. Terry McDermott hit the Super Cup's first final hat-trick and Kenny Dalglish, Keegan's replacement, was also among the scorers. The next year, however, Liverpool lost in the final to Anderlecht after the Reds made it hard for themselves by losing the first leg in Belgium 3-1. Despite starting the concluding instalment encouragingly with an early Emlyn Hughes goal, Rob Rensenbrink's equaliser – his second strike over the two legs – ultimately proved decisive as Liverpool could only manage a 2-1 win on the night through David Fairclough's late effort.

In a final that wasn't played until early 1980 because the sides could not come up with suitable dates before the end of 1979, Forest overcame Barcelona 2-1 on aggregate. Former Arsenal favourite Charlie George gave them a 1-0 lead from the first leg at the City Ground and Scottish defender Kenny Burns emerged as an unlikely hero at the Camp Nou with an equaliser. Forest defended their title as European champions by beating Keegan's Hamburg in Madrid's Bernabéu through wily winger John Robertson's solo goal. But later that year, Valencia – having beaten Arsenal – claimed a double over the English as they beat Forest in the Super Cup on the away goals rule after a 2-2 aggregate draw.

Forest also lost the 1980 Intercontinental Cup, a forerunner to the FIFA Club World Cup, in which the European Cup winners were pitted against the champions of South America, as they went down 1-0 to Uruguay's Nacional. Both Liverpool and Forest had declined to take part in the showpiece in 1977 and 1979 and, in between when Liverpool would have qualified for the final as European champions for the second year running, neither they nor runners-up Club Bruges made themselves available, so there was no competition.

* * *

The vast majority of England's most successful clubs in the 1970s, when foreign players were still a rarity on the domestic scene, benefited enormously from the talents of Scots, Welsh and Irish.

Yet the Everton side who won the opening First Division title of the decade by a convincing margin of nine points were packed with Englishmen and managed by one in Darlington-born Harry Catterick. World Cup winner Alan Ball was one of the famous 'Holy Trinity' in midfield at Goodison Park alongside Howard Kendall and Colin Harvey. In defence, centre-back Brian Labone and full-backs Tommy Wright and Keith Newton were Ball's England team-mates at the World Cup in Mexico that summer, while goalkeeper Gordon West had won three caps in the late 1960s and centre-forward Joe Royle would be capped, along with Harvey, in early 1971.

Everton's second appearance in the European Cup in 1970/71 saw them profit from the introduction of penalty shoot-outs when, in the second round, they beat Borussia Mönchengladbach after both legs had ended in 1-1 draws. Royle failed to convert from the spot, but Ball and Kendall were among those successful as Everton won 4-3 on penalties at Goodison. Catterick's side then bowed out on the away goals rule to eventual finalists Panathinaikos in the quarter-finals. Future England striker David Johnson snatched a last-ditch leveller on Merseyside for a 1-1 draw, but the second leg ended goalless. It was this season that Arsenal won only the second 'double' in the history of the Football League, ten years after north London rivals Tottenham had claimed the first. The Gunners held off the challenge of Leeds to clinch the title and beat Liverpool in the FA Cup Final.

Early that season, the English fighting spirit in Europe came to the fore. Arsenal were Fairs Cup holders after beating Anderlecht in the previous season when they overturned a 3-1 first-leg deficit: Ray Kennedy pulled a crucial late goal back in Brussels before England forward John Radford was among the scorers in a 3-0 win at Highbury in the second leg. The Gunners launched their defence of the trophy with a first-round tie against Italian big guns Lazio, but after a bruising encounter which ended in a 2-2 draw, the sides dished out more harm to each other at a post-match meal together, when Arsenal were drawn into a brawl with their opponents.

Unwisely, they were all invited to meet up in a Rome restaurant. Future England international Kennedy, who a little under seven years later would celebrate in the Eternal City with Liverpool when they won the European Cup, was involved in an altercation with one of the Lazio players outside the eatery. The incident escalated when fans of the hosts joined in what became a street fight. Even Arsenal manager Bertie Mee, a man of great dignity and certainly not one regarded as being confrontational, stepped into the fray before police arrived to quell the skirmish. Arsenal won the second leg at Highbury 2-0 and it was Kennedy who scored the goal that rubber-stamped the league title for the Gunners – at Tottenham, of all places.

Scots also brought shine to Arsenal's dual silver lining of 1971. Skipper Frank McLintock was at the heart of defence, Bob Wilson in goal, and George Graham commanding in midfield. Northern Ireland right-back Pat Rice was another stalwart of Mee's side. Arsenal's first foray into the European Cup was over by the quarter-final stage where they lost to holders – and ultimate winners again – Ajax 3-1 on aggregate. Kennedy gave the Gunners the lead in the first leg in Amsterdam, but they lost 2-1 and then faced too much of an uphill struggle at Highbury after Graham's early own goal.

The Liverpool line-up beaten by Arsenal at Wembley in the 1971 FA Cup Final had a new name in their ranks at the start of the next season: Kevin Keegan had been plucked from the obscurity of Scunthorpe United and a star was born. With one European trophy under their belts, Liverpool went in search of the big prize at continental level in the 1973/74 campaign, but were undone in the second round by Yugoslavia's Red Star Belgrade. Right-back Chris Lawler, who had made all four of his England appearances in 1971, was Liverpool's scorer in both legs as Red Star recorded carbon-copy 2-1 victories. McDermott made such an impression for Newcastle in their 3-0 FA Cup Final defeat by Liverpool in 1974 that the Reds took him back to his native Merseyside later in the calendar year. And in 1977, the midfielder, soon to become an England international (co-scorers Tommy Smith and Phil Neal were already capped), struck the opener in Liverpool's 3-1 European Cup Final victory over Mönchengladbach at Rome's Olympic Stadium, in a fitting farewell to Keegan.

The chance of a then-unprecedented 'treble' of winning the First Division, FA Cup and European Cup had eluded Liverpool four days earlier when they lost to bitter rivals Manchester United (who achieved the three-trophy feat in 1999 as did Manchester City in 2023) in the FA Cup Final.

Liverpool, though, bounced back in some style. Republic of Ireland forward Steve Heighway slipped a perfect ball into the path of McDermott, whose first-time finish found the far corner of the net to hand Liverpool a 28th-minute lead. After Danish forward Allan Simonsen's cracking 52nd-minute leveller, defender Smith – on his 600th Liverpool appearance – was a surprise scorer with a bullet header at the near post on the end of Heighway's left-wing corner in the 65th minute. Right-back Neal then sealed the success with a penalty seven minutes from time after Keegan's burst into the middle of the box ended with him tumbling under West Germany right-back Berti Vogts's high-risk challenge. The occasion was enough to convince tough-tackling Merseysider Smith, nicknamed 'The Anfield Iron', to delay plans to end his long association with Liverpool.

But England captain Keegan headed for a new life with Hamburg and Paisley signed Celtic and Scotland forward Dalglish for a record fee between British clubs of £440,000 to fill the void. A year on and it was much more of a Scottish affair for Liverpool, Dalglish scoring the only goal as the Reds retained the trophy against Bruges at Wembley. Dalglish's compatriot, Graeme Souness, had joined Liverpool from Middlesbrough in January of that season, and it was the midfield strongman who provided the slick assist for Dalglish to finish. The side that started the game also included Scotland centre-back Alan Hansen, while Heighway came off the bench and Wales left-back Joey Jones was also among the substitutes. A year earlier, both players had started against Borussia, who fell victims to Liverpool again in the semi-finals of 1978. It was a curious coincidence that Liverpool's first two trophies in Europe were won against the sides they beat in the same sequence in those European Cup finals – Borussia in the 1973 UEFA Cup and Bruges in that competition three years later. In both years, of course, Liverpool were also Football League champions.

There was a false start against Borussia in 1973 when the first leg at Anfield was abandoned after only 27 minutes due to torrential rain on an already heavy surface. As was the way in those days, the game was rearranged for the following May evening and Liverpool were 3-0 winners, with Keegan scoring twice before half-time and England centre-back Larry Lloyd adding the third goal on the hour. In the second leg in West Germany, where again there was a deluge, Liverpool lost 2-0 on the night to a Jupp Heynckes double, but just did enough to hold on to their aggregate lead. The victory over Bruges in 1976 was also earned the hard way as the Reds came out 4-3 winners on aggregate after recovering from the shock of going two down in the first 15 minutes at Anfield. Kennedy, Jimmy Case and Keegan, with a penalty, turned the tie on its head after the break. In the second leg, Keegan was key again with a quick-fire reply on the quarter-hour after Belgium striker Raoul Lambert, who had netted Bruges' opener in the first leg after only five minutes, converted an 11th-minute spot kick.

When it comes to English top-flight titles in the 1970s, next to Liverpool only Derby County won more than one. They were First Division champions in 1972 under Clough and in 1975 when Scottish legend – and former Rams and Tottenham skipper – Dave Mackay was in charge. A core of those who had been triumphant under Clough were augmented by the likes of former England forward Lee and Scotland midfielder Bruce Rioch. Charlie George was signed from Arsenal and scored a hat-trick in a famous 4-1 home win over Real Madrid in the second round of the 1975/76 European Cup. In a remarkable comeback, however, Real overturned the deficit at the Bernabéu, winning 5-1.

Clough's Derby had reached the semi-finals of the European Cup in 1973, when they were eliminated by Italian giants Juventus in controversial circumstances as hostilities between two proud footballing nations boiled over again. It was said that John Charles, the Leeds and Juventus legend, had tipped off Clough's assistant, Peter Taylor, before the match in Turin that he had spotted Juve's West German striker Helmut Haller – scorer of the opening goal of the 1966 World Cup Final – going into the dressing room of referee Gerhard Schulenburg. The obvious suggestion was that Haller had tried to influence his fellow countryman. At half-time, Haller headed for the official's room once more, but as he did so he found Taylor on his tail and gave him the brushoff in the form of a sharp dig in the ribs.

Derby, repeatedly penalised for fouls, had their suspicions raised when Roy McFarland and Archie Gemmill, two players booked in previous rounds, were cautioned and therefore ruled out of the return match through suspension. The Rams lost 3-1 before being held to a goalless draw in the second leg. Clough claimed the first game was fixed and, in a characteristically colourful outburst, rebuked the hosts when Italian journalists congregated outside Derby's dressing room in search of post-match reaction. UEFA held an investigation into the game in Italy, but failed to turn up any evidence to support Clough's assertions.

Haller, however, had been on the losing side when Leeds beat Juventus in 1971 in the last Fairs Cup before the competition was given its makeover. The first attempt to play the first leg in Turin was abandoned after 51 minutes due to a waterlogged pitch. When the game was rescheduled for two days later, Leeds drew 2-2 with goals by newly capped England defender Paul Madeley and midfielder Mick Bates, while Roberto Bettega and future Italy team-mate – and future England manager – Fabio Capello netted for Juve. England's Allan Clarke scored in the second leg at Elland Road, Pietro Anastasi replying, but Don Revie's men, who had beaten Liverpool over two legs in the semi-finals, lifted the trophy for the second time on the away goals rule.

Five years later, Revie was on the receiving end as England manager when Italy won 2-0 in a World Cup qualifier in Rome. The contrast in fortunes between England's national team and club sides was not lost on Italy's manager, Enzo Bearzot, who told the visiting media he 'watched 20 English league fixtures' in preparation, and added, 'They have all been very good and I have been impressed with the standard of play. I wish I could get all the spirit and fight of English players into my team. I told them as much in my pre-match briefing. But your international team does not play like your English club teams play. I am very surprised.'

* * *

In the Derby squad of 1972, there was a smattering of Scots and Welsh. John McGovern, a Scot, was one of Clough's disciples, playing under him at Hartlepool, Derby, Leeds and Nottingham Forest. McGovern skippered Forest to their First Division title triumph and European Cup Final victories of 1979 and 1980.

The Derby side he played in included fellow Scots Gemmill and John O'Hare. Like co-midfielder McGovern, Gemmill and striker O'Hare would follow Clough to Forest. Wales were represented among the Rams by midfielder Alan Durban and midfielder-cum-defender Terry Hennessey. Gifted left-winger Alan Hinton was a former England international, while striker Kevin Hector was bound for such status. When Derby's first title was confirmed, it was once again Revie's Leeds – another side of the '70s with a rich mix of British and Irish – who finished as runners-up. Derby skipper McFarland and fellow defender Colin Todd, who had both returned from the team's end-of-season trip to Majorca to prepare for England duty, had limited time to celebrate as they were due to link up with Ramsey's squad for the European Championship quarter-final second leg against West Germany in Berlin. McGovern's goal in a 1-0 win against Liverpool at the Baseball Ground had put Derby in pole position and when, a week later, the Reds – in the title race themselves – were held at Highbury by reigning champions Arsenal, the defeat of Leeds by Wolves on the same night at Molineux saw the coronation of the Rams as kings of England.

It was another bitter pill for Leeds. Like all of the eminent sides of that time, they were blessed with top English talent blended with outstanding Scots, like skipper Billy Bremner, wide men Peter Lorimer and Eddie Gray and Republic of Ireland schemer Johnny Giles, who formed a formidable partnership with his captain in the middle of the pitch. There was also the Wales goalkeeper, Gary Sprake, whose habit of making mistakes ultimately cost him his place to Scotland's David Harvey, while another Welshman, Terry Yorath, and Gray's younger brother and fellow Scot, Frank, were valued utility players. An impressive defensive department featured England internationals in Paul Reaney, Jack Charlton, Norman Hunter, Terry Cooper and the versatile Madeley. The established front two were also England men, Clarke and Mick Jones. After the agony of a third consecutive season as runners-up, Leeds would have to wait a further two years to regain the First Division title when they deposed Liverpool, who had to settle for second place themselves on that occasion. It was a triumphant swansong for Revie as he quit Elland Road to become England manager.

Clough proved a controversial – and short-lived – successor, but Leeds' first post-Revie season ended with Jimmy Armfield, their third manager inside a year, leading them to the highly contentious European Cup Final at the Parc des Princes in Paris, where they lost 2-0 to reigning champions Bayern Munich. Furious Leeds fans rioted, claiming their side had been robbed of glory. There was no real question that Leeds, the better team on the night, were denied two first-half penalties – and it was England nemesis Franz Beckenbauer who was the chief protagonist. The Bayern and West Germany captain was twice given the benefit of the doubt by French referee Michel Kitabdjian. First, the ball struck the grounded Beckenbauer on an arm as Lorimer tried to skip past him. Then, Beckenbauer scythed down Clarke in the box, but escaped punishment.

In the second half, Lorimer lashed home a trademark volley when the ball dropped to him following a Giles free kick, but Beckenbauer complained to the referee and, after it seemed a goal had been given, it was suddenly ruled out for a marginal offside against Bremner. Franz Roth then gave Bayern an undeserved lead in the 71st minute and, ten minutes later, West Germany striker Gerd Müller – another old scourge of England – scored the second. Riot police were called in as the Leeds supporters ripped out and hurled seats and other objects. The trouble resulted in the club being banned from Europe for four years, though the sanction was halved on appeal. Due to Leeds' subsequent fall from grace in the wake of Revie's departure, the ban was never brought into force.

It was not the only time Leeds were embroiled in controversy abroad. In the final of the 1973 European Cup Winners' Cup they lost to AC Milan in Salonika, where Hunter was sent off late in the game after retaliating angrily to a cynical kick from Italian international midfielder Gianni Rivera, and Leeds complained bitterly about key decisions by Greek referee Christos Michas, who was later banned by UEFA. There were parallels with the game against Bayern, as Leeds – weakened by the absence of Bremner, Giles, Clarke and Eddie Gray – should have been awarded a penalty when

Jones was clearly tripped and also had a spot kick appeal for handball waved away. Furthermore, the only goal of the game, Luciano Chiarugi's free kick in the opening minutes, should have been indirect, insisted Leeds, who lodged an unsuccessful appeal for a rematch.

Clough's first game as Leeds manager, the 1974 Charity Shield at Wembley against Liverpool, produced not-too-dissimilar scenes when Keegan and Bremner fought and were both sent off. Discarding their shirts as they left the field was viewed as a further disgrace. The trouble all began when the wily Giles floored Keegan and escaped with only a booking from referee Bob Matthewson. Moments later, after an off-the-ball incident and with Clough sitting uncomfortably next to the retirement-bound Shankly at pitchside, Keegan and Bremner were banished and ultimately both banned for 11 matches as the FA decided to make an example of the pair against the background of growing concern over football's image, which was already becoming tarnished by the hooliganism of the game's so-called fans.

It was an ominous start for Clough in the Leeds job, but greater glories still lay ahead for 'Old Big 'Ead'. It was in 1975 that he made an inspired move to the City Ground, where Derby's bitter rivals Nottingham Forest were going nowhere in the Second Division. Yet within two years, in tandem with assistant Peter Taylor, he had them promoted – and in their first season back in the First Division, they topped the lot for the first time in their history.

Clough recruited and promoted the best of British, examples being England keeper Peter Shilton, Three Lions forward Trevor Francis – Britain's first £1m player – and right-back Viv Anderson, who broke into the international side along with strikers Tony Woodcock and Garry Birtles, the latter having to wait until 1980 for his first cap. The manager was also reunited on the banks of the River Trent with McGovern, Gemmill and O'Hare from his Derby days, and made players of two other Scots in Robertson and Burns. A solid central-defensive partnership was formed between the unsung Burns and former Liverpool man Lloyd, whose England career would be surprisingly revived as a result, while Frank Gray was brought in from Leeds. Northern Ireland midfielder Martin O'Neill was also part of the East Midlands club's astonishing success.

It was Francis who produced a diving header on the end of Robertson's left-wing centre to cap Forest's fairy-tale journey with victory over Swedish side Malmö in the European Cup Final in Munich's Olympiastadion in 1979.

8

The Revolutionary Revie

DON REVIE was one of the most divisive figures in English football, in many ways a man of contradictions. He became England manager in July 1974 after being identified by the Football Association as the long-term successor to World Cup winner Sir Alf Ramsey.

The departure of Ramsey and arrival of Revie proved a ludicrously protracted process. After England's draw with Poland at Wembley in October 1973 and consequent failure to qualify for the 1974 World Cup, Ramsey's days were numbered. But days would become weeks, and weeks would become months – six in all – before Ramsey was finally shown the door. The FA's dithering had left them with a problem. Finding a suitable replacement at that time of year, the closing weeks of the football season, was virtually impossible. So in came the avuncular Joe Mercer to hold the reins as caretaker manager before Revie assumed control for what was to be the beginning of arguably the most turbulent three years in England's history.

At the time, Leeds boss Revie had recently led his side to their second top-flight title and was one of the country's managerial heavyweights alongside the likes of Brian Clough, a fellow son of Middlesbrough and a major bugbear, who would succeed him at Elland Road and last only 44 days in the job. After Clough's brief tenure came to an abrupt end, the pair went head-to-head in an enthralling Yorkshire Television debate chaired by journalist, and later Labour MP, Austin Mitchell.

It was a fascinating duel between two of the titans of the game. Clough, always a natural in front of the TV cameras and with a smile playing on his lips for much of the discussion, was far more at ease than rival Revie. The argument Clough propounded for taking the Leeds job was largely reasoned, if clearly ultimately misguided. Revie, on the other hand, appeared uncomfortable, pensive and undeniably defensive for the most part. He had recommended to the Leeds board that wily midfield schemer Johnny Giles would be the best man to succeed him. The interview became increasingly combative and, at one stage, Revie seemed to be genuinely rattled. Clough even eventually managed to extract agreement from Revie on some of the points he made so forcefully during the exchanges.

It was clear, and Clough admitted as much in the course of the conversation, that his chief motivation for wanting to take over Revie's mantle at Leeds was attempting to better his predecessor's achievements with them. Winning the European Cup – as Clough did in 1979 and 1980 as manager of Nottingham Forest – would have been one of his principal priorities. Yet it was Clough's successor, former England captain Jimmy Armfield, who took Leeds to the European Cup Final at the end of the 1974/75 season, when they were beaten 2-0 by holders Bayern Munich in Paris in a highly controversial contest marred by violent crowd disorder.

When all was said and done between Clough and Revie, the inescapable truth was, even though they hailed from the same neck of the woods and may have appeared to hold many other things in common – both had been forwards, both had played for England and both had played for Sunderland – they were very different characters who did not see eye-to-eye; it was deeply personal. We will never know whether Clough would have succeeded in his aim of eclipsing Revie at Elland Road. What we do know, however, is that, all too soon for his liking, Clough discovered he could not shake off the legacy of Revie, who had made Leeds what they were.

Having become their player-manager in March 1961, under two and a half years after joining them from Sunderland, Revie had begun to transform a then-Second Division club who had never won a major honour. He introduced a pure, all-white strip in the style of the mighty Real Madrid, discarding the last vestiges of the predominantly blue and gold colours they had worn for many years. That, in itself, seemed a statement of Revie's intent, although there have been suggestions that the change was because he believed, with a certain logic, that white was easier to pick out when it came to locating a team-mate.

Leeds were promoted as champions in 1964, with Revie's former club Sunderland runners-up after a ferocious and ill-tempered struggle between them. The seeds of that rivalry were sown in 1958 when Revie was said to have come to blows with Sunderland manager Alan Brown in a dispute after a game at Rotherham that turned out to be the forward's last for the club. And the animosity grew early in the 1962/63 season after Bobby Collins, the terrier-like Leeds midfielder, broke the leg of Sunderland's Willie McPheat with a scandalously high tackle. When Brown – a disciplinarian from whom Revie had learned much and a mentor on Wearside to a young Clough – shocked the Rokerites by quitting for Sheffield Wednesday shortly before Sunderland made their return to top-flight action, they put George Hardwick in temporary charge. But their poor start to the season did not go unnoticed by Revie. While his Leeds side were soon thriving in the big time, he was unhappy that the club had stopped short of offering him the long-term contract he was seeking to guarantee greater job security.

Revie applied for the vacancy at Sunderland, but after crisis talks Leeds decided to accede to their manager's wishes and handed him the deal he wanted, with a pay rise. Anything else would have patently been folly. Leeds made an enormous and immediate impact in the First Division, only losing the title race to Manchester United on goal average and underlining their emergence by reaching their first FA Cup Final, in which they lost to Liverpool after extra time. They followed that in 1966 with another second-place finish in the First Division, this time to the men from Anfield. But Leeds were title winners in 1969, the year after they won their first two major trophies: the League Cup – Terry Cooper's screamer the sole goal against Arsenal – and then the Inter-Cities Fairs Cup, in which they overcame Ferencváros over two legs and again with a single strike, courtesy of Mick Jones at Elland Road, to atone for defeat by Dinamo Zagreb in the final the previous year. The Fairs Cup was won again in 1971 against Juventus, and the following year Leeds lifted the FA Cup for the first time in their history in the centenary final, beating Arsenal with Allan Clarke's diving header, on the end of a cross by fellow England forward Jones, producing a repeat of the result between the teams at Wembley in 1968.

As ever as it seemed with Revie's Leeds, however, it was a bittersweet occasion. Jones suffered a dislocated left elbow in the dying moments of the match and memorably, swathed in bandages, made a painful walk up the steps to the Royal Box with the help of team-mate Norman Hunter to receive his winners' medal. For once, Leeds had the sympathy vote to go with the silverware.

Success rarely came easily to Revie and his men, who were often football's bridesmaids. In 1970, as well as losing the marathon FA Cup Final with Chelsea – the replay of which witnessed the Blues more than match Leeds' reputation for physicality – they missed out on the First Division title as runners-up to Everton. And they were pipped to the crown by Arsenal the next year as the Gunners won the First Division and FA Cup double. Revie's wretched luck was crystallised in a crucial game at home to West Bromwich Albion. With Colin Suggett in an offside position, Tony Brown blocked Hunter's ball and broke forward to tee up Jeff Astle to score. Referee Ray Tinkler then found himself in the eye of a storm as Leeds players and fans responded furiously to the decision – or 'non-decision' as the BBC's *Match of the Day* commentator Barry Davies described it. Tinkler needed police protection with fans invading the pitch and Davies captured Revie's reaction perfectly, referring to the Leeds manager 'looking up to the heavens in disgust' after ushering the linesman, who had raised his flag but been dismissed by the referee, on to the pitch in the forlorn hope of salvaging the situation. Leeds lost and the title nightmare stretched to a third consecutive season when that man Clough and his Derby County side, like Arsenal, beat them to the championship by a point, with the FA Cup providing some consolation for Revie.

But the next year, 1973, firm favourites Leeds were humbled in one of the biggest shocks of all time. Second Division Sunderland, managed by Bob Stokoe – another of Revie's old adversaries – beat them in the FA Cup Final, Ian Porterfield scoring the only goal of the game and Black Cats goalkeeper Jim Montgomery performing with feline agility in making a miraculous double save to deny Trevor Cherry and Peter Lorimer. Stokoe was, in part, fuelled by the resentment he felt towards Revie, who he accused of trying to fix a Leeds match against Bury in 1962. Revie's side were threatened with relegation from the Second Division, and Stokoe, who was Bury boss, said his rival offered a sum of money to go 'easy' in the game at Gigg Lane. There were more allegations of match-fixing against Revie – notably by former Leeds keeper Gary Sprake – but those who were closest to him were steadfast in their rebuttals of the claims.

Controversy, however, was Revie's constant companion. Only 11 days after losing to Sunderland, Leeds were beaten by AC Milan in a stormy European Cup Winners' Cup Final in Greece as they protested about the fiercely disputed free kick which proved decisive. Yet even before the double disappointment in the cup competitions, Revie was growing restless. So much so, in fact, that he met Everton chairman John Moores on the eve of Leeds' departure for Greece. Irrespective of the injustices Leeds met with against Milan, did Revie commit the cardinal football sin and take his eye off the ball? In other words, had being courted by Everton, who were looking for a new manager after Harry Catterick had accepted lighter duties due to health issues, been a distraction for Revie? It seems that was the case as it is common knowledge he had admitted to his players, who still performed well against Milan, his intention to leave.

Everton were prepared to tempt Revie with an opening offer said to be worth £20,000 a year, more than he was earning at Leeds. Ultimately, however, Revie remained in West Yorkshire and his side eventually recovered from those two devastating defeats. The reward for all was the return of the Football League championship trophy to Elland Road in 1974, with Leeds losing only four of their 42 league games that season. Then England came calling and, after agonising over whether to stay with the Whites for one last crack at the elusive European Cup, their patriarchal manager did opt to leave, returning to the international arena where he had won six caps as a forward.

In the modern game, there is the 'false nine', a position that has its roots in what was known as the 'Revie Plan' when the man himself was the first to adopt the role of deep-lying centre-forward in his Manchester City days in the 1950s. Revie had a revolutionary zeal about him and always seemed to be at the heart of change. Although he inspired unswerving loyalty among his Leeds charges, in the wider football world Revie was, as the title of Richard Sutcliffe's authorised biography said, 'revered and reviled'. Mud sticks, they say, and the 'dirty Leeds' tag certainly stuck. There could be no equivocation when it came to their ruthlessness, but equally none would question their brilliance.

Both those facets of Leeds' game were witnessed in their memorable 7-0 slaughter of Southampton at Elland Road in March 1972 – on the back of a 5-1 home hammering of Manchester United. Revie's men played keep-ball, stringing together 39 passes at one point, as they toyed with the tormented Saints. Still, that sort of form was not enough to see off the title challenge of Clough's Derby, whose 2-0 defeat of Leeds at the Baseball Ground on April Fool's Day was, in the end, decisive.

Like him or loathe him, Revie was very much one of the game's innovators, proof of which were the fabled dossiers that were compiled on opponents in his Leeds days, with the help of key backroom man Syd Owen. Such thorough preparation exhibited Revie's determination to be ahead of the rest in every respect and it was that forensic approach which conflicted with the allegations of match-fixing.

Whichever way he was perceived, by 1974 England needed a new direction. And with it came a new look as Revie re-established links with sportswear manufacturer Admiral, who had supplied Leeds, to produce a fresh England kit. Out went the old, traditional, white shirts and navy shorts and in came white shirts and royal-blue shorts with trimmings featuring royal blue and red. The colours of the Union flag were not to everyone's liking, with many Englishmen complaining that it was too much a reflection of the United Kingdom as a whole. But there were more important matters at hand, notably the serious business of trying to qualify for the 1976 European Championship.

9

Highs and Lows

DON REVIE'S tenure as England manager began in earnest against Czechoslovakia at Wembley on 30 September 1974. Perhaps surprisingly given the lacklustre draw against Yugoslavia, he only made three changes to the starting line-up. Less surprising was that two of the switches saw the return of two disciples from his Leeds United days: Paul Madeley and Norman Hunter. The other player brought in by Revie was Gerry Francis, the cultured Queens Park Rangers midfielder, who was making his international debut at only 22.

Before the match, lyric sheets, on which were printed the words of 'Land of Hope and Glory', were distributed to the crowd, while the decision for England to adopt a new strip added to the feeling that this was very much the beginning of a new era for the national side. Revie could not have wished for a better way to start as England manager, though he did have to wait until the second half for his side to break through the Czechoslovak defence. In the 64th minute, he threw on Trevor Brooking and debutant Dave Thomas, and seven minutes later the latter supplied a cross for Mick Channon, who had missed a good opportunity in the first half, to score with a fine header. Two great finishes by Colin Bell shortly afterwards – his first and only brace in an international shirt – gave England a 3-0 victory and their biggest win in over a year. As the game drew to a close and 'Land of Hope and Glory' echoed around Wembley, it appeared as though the FA had perhaps pulled off a masterstroke by appointing Revie.

England's final opponents of 1974 were Portugal, who had coincidentally been the first side they played that year. There is a plethora of adages in football, though one of the more common in relation to management did not cross Revie's mind when he named his side for his second match: don't change a winning team. Sure enough, the changes he made did not have the desired effect. Terry Cooper, another of his old Leeds boys, came off injured after only 24 minutes in what would be his final appearance for England, while Elland Road colleague Allan Clarke was also substituted. Brooking and Thomas started, as a disjointed England only managed a goalless draw against the Portuguese. There were audible boos as Revie's men trudged down the tunnel at full time in what was a stark contrast to their reception just three weeks earlier.

Their first game of 1975 was not until 12 March against World Cup holders West Germany. The friendly had been organised to celebrate England's 100th match at Wembley, and the FA had understandably selected the opponents they had beaten in their most famous victory. This game was arguably the first occasion that truly displayed Revie's willingness to chop and change his side as he named three debutants: Leicester City right-back Steve Whitworth, QPR left-back Ian Gillard and Stoke City midfielder Alan Hudson. West Germany were in something of a transitional period at the time with Gerd Müller and Wolfgang Overath having played their last games for their country, while Paul Breitner was another that England did not have to worry about. The Germans had, however, maintained a strong spine to the team with Sepp Maier in goal and the formidable Franz Beckenbauer at the heart of defence. One of the major talking points before the game was not just the return of Alan Ball to the England team, but also the decision to hand him the captain's armband. Newcastle striker Malcolm Macdonald was also back in the side after being recalled by Revie.

After a strong spell of pressure from England in the opening period, West German defender Bernhard Cullmann hacked down Whitworth, and Bell scored with the help of a deflection from Hudson's right-wing free kick. In the second half, Bell was inches from another goal when he followed up after an uncertain Maier only parried Macdonald's effort and then got just enough on the ball to take it wide of the far post. English nerves were settled in the 66th minute when Macdonald, who had tested Maier more than once, scored his first goal for his country. Channon was fouled and took a quick free kick to release Ball on the right, and his cross sailed beyond Maier's reach to be met by Macdonald with a far-post header. England were dominant throughout the game, well worth their 2-0 win, and their performance was all the more impressive considering the abject state of a rain-softened pitch.

England returned to Wembley the following month and registered a 5-0 win over Cyprus in a European Championship qualifier, with Macdonald scoring all five goals. Another of the standout performers of England's first two games of the year was Hudson, who had created the opening goals in both matches. Despite two good showings, Hudson remarkably never played for England again. He would move to Arsenal the following year, though he would only play for the Gunners for two seasons before heading to the United States.

There were plenty of positives from Revie's opening four games. Though the draw with Portugal meant that he had not achieved a 100 per cent start, England's defence were performing well and they were yet to concede a goal under their new boss. Despite a string of clean sheets, Revie decided to tinker with his defence once again for the visit to Cyprus on 11 May. The right-back position had for spells been held by Madeley, Peter Storey, Emlyn Hughes, David Nish and Mick Mills in the two years preceding Revie's appointment, yet he was impressed enough with Whitworth's performance against West Germany to award him a prolonged run in the team. Francis, having won his first senior caps in Revie's opening two games in charge, had hoped for a recall in the game against Cyprus. The midfielder told ITV's *The Big Match*, 'Having seen the pictures of the pitch a while back, I wouldn't have believed that the game could have gone on, considering the chaos there. But obviously Don Revie and the Football Association have been over there to see the pitch, the facilities and security, etc., and it seems to be going ahead.' The 'chaos' Francis was referring to was the fallout from the Turkish invasion of Cyprus in 1974 which had left hundreds of thousands displaced. The Turks had invaded in response to a Greek-led coup in Cyprus, and tensions still remained high a year later. As it happened, Francis had to wait until the visit of Wales to Wembley the following month in the British Home Championship for a return to Revie's ever-changing line-up.

Coming just a month after that home hammering of Cyprus, England were expected to once more win by a large margin, but they had to make do with a 1-0 victory thanks to an early goal from Kevin Keegan. The pitch in Limassol was in a poor state with many patches of the surface totally devoid of grass, which did more to help the home side than the visitors. Dennis Tueart, then of Manchester City, was England's only debutant, coming on as a substitute for Keegan in the later stages of the game.

The result was hardly eye-catching, but it left England with an excellent chance of qualifying for the final stages of the European Championship. Portugal had been pulled apart 5-0 by Czechoslovakia 11 days before England's second victory over Cyprus, while the Cypriots themselves were already all but out of contention. England at this stage topped the group having only dropped a point. With just two games left to play, England appeared to be nearing the end of their tournament exile. Neither of these fixtures, however, was to be played at Wembley, a fact which the squad knew was to their detriment. On the other hand, UEFA had decided that England would host the tournament were they to make it to the next stage, meaning the Three Lions were presented with the opportunity to play a semi-final of a major competition in front of an expectant Wembley crowd.

In the first of England's Home Championship matches that year, they faced Northern Ireland on 17 May. Before the game, Keegan received a death threat from an individual claiming to be a member of the IRA. Revie gave the Liverpool man the option of sitting the game out, but Keegan opted to play. Ipswich Town midfielder Colin Viljoen made his debut for England. Born in Johannesburg, South Africa, Viljoen had only become eligible to play for England four years prior to his first appearance for them. The two seasons that followed his call-up would be blighted with ill fortune: he suffered an injury to his Achilles tendon and was not included in Ipswich's 1978 FA Cup Final-winning side. Though England created enough chances to beat Northern Ireland, the game finished 0-0. Following the below-par showing at Windsor Park, it was only a small comfort to Revie that his side had managed a record-breaking six clean sheets in a row and were still yet to concede a goal under his charge. This run of shut-outs, however, would come to an end in their next game of the Home Championship against an inspired Wales.

Many players – Harry Kane, Darius Vassell and Marcus Rashford, to name but three – have scored on their debuts for England, but those who have notched multiple goals on their first appearance for the Three Lions are members of a far more select group. David Johnson was in fine form for Ipswich when Revie picked him to lead the line against the Welsh. After just eight minutes, the ball fell kindly to the moustachioed forward to head into an empty net following a mix-up in the opposition's defence. Wales, however, regrouped after the restart, and John Toshack equalised from close range after Ray Clemence had failed to push a shot away from danger. The Wembley crowd were all the more shocked when Arfon Griffiths put the Welsh in front. Brian Little – another player making his debut – came off the bench as England pressed and for a while it appeared as though Wales were heading for what would have been a famous victory. In the 85th minute, however, Little put a superb floating cross into the box. Dai Davies made an ill-judged decision to come off his line in an attempt to deal with the threat, and Johnson was on hand to meet the ball and head over the onrushing keeper.

Keegan, for the second game running, made the headlines, but this time for a very different reason. Along with Bell, Keegan had been left out of the team that played Wales, his omission leading to him leaving the squad's hotel and returning home. Revie was able to convince Keegan to come back for the final game of the Home Championship, explaining that he had left him off the team sheet simply because he wanted to keep him fresh for the clash with Scotland. In his time as England manager, it was not unusual for Revie to give no reason to a player as to why he had been dropped, and this was not the first or last instance of him upsetting one of his star men.

Having drawn their last two games, England went into the showdown against Scotland knowing that they needed to win if they wanted to lift the trophy. With both Bell and

Keegan restored to the team, Revie secured what was arguably his greatest victory as an international manager. Francis put them ahead in the fifth minute with a fabulous shot that was struck so well that Stewart Kennedy, the Scotland keeper, did not even attempt a save. Then, a well-worked counterattack led to Keegan supplying a cross for Kevin Beattie to put England two goals to the good. Bell scored with a long-range strike before Bruce Rioch pulled a goal back for the Scots from the penalty spot. The 3-1 scoreline at half-time was perhaps harsh on Scotland who had played well for long spells. However, their undoing had been their inability to deal with England's counterattacking play. Francis's second of the game was just as good as his first: a free kick from 30 yards was teed up for the QPR man to smash the ball in off a post. Scotland's humiliation was completed by Johnson, the forward scoring from a rebound after Dave Watson's attempt had cannoned off the frame of the goal.

To date, England's 5-1 victory on 24 May 1975 remains one of their greatest wins over their bitter rivals (though it did not match the record win against Scotland, 9-3 at Wembley 14 years earlier). Few must have known at the time that the game would also represent the end of an era. It would be Ball's final appearance in an England shirt, even though he had only been made captain by Revie four games earlier, making the Scotland match also the last time any of the players who figured for England in the 1966 World Cup Final would play for their country. Ball was just 30 when he was discarded by Revie.

Lifting the Home Championship trophy had kept the critics at bay, though it was evident that they would become more vocal if England did not perform in their final three games of the year. There was a gap of nearly four months between England's fixtures, and they did not return to action until 3 September. A friendly away to Switzerland presented

Revie with the opportunity to try out new players ahead of two European Championship qualifiers. Yet, perhaps surprisingly, he made only one change with Tony Currie coming in for Ball. There were plenty of strong characters in the England squad, meaning the captain's armband could have potentially been handed to several players. Gerry Francis, one of the youngest in the team, was given the honour on just his fifth appearance for England.

Keegan scored in the eighth minute against the Swiss and three minutes later he had a chance to add to his tally from the penalty spot, but his effort was saved. England did not, however, have to wait long for a second goal. Channon scored his first of the year at international level, but Servette forward Kudi Müller halved the deficit shortly afterwards. There were no further changes to the scoreline, all three goals coming in the first half an hour of the match. Though England had not played with the same panache that they had shown against Scotland, they had put in a workmanlike display against Switzerland, and Revie's record of nine played and none lost appeared to place them in good stead going into their encounter with Czechoslovakia. However, in spite of the solid outing in Basel, Revie once again decided that changes were needed. Never the most cautious of managers, Revie was renowned for his attacking style of play, but the team he named to take on the Czechoslovaks bordered on recklessness. A front three of Clarke, Macdonald and Channon were fielded with Keegan and Bell supporting them.

England's biggest battle of the scheduled matchday proved to be against the elements. A dense fog fell on Bratislava, and although the referee allowed the game to start, it was abandoned after less than 20 minutes. It was quickly decided that the fixture should be played the following day, which meant the squad had to face another 24 hours behind the Iron Curtain. For the fourth successive game, England opened the scoring: Keegan, after completing a mazy run, clipped the ball into the box for Channon to chip home on 27 minutes. The equaliser from Zdeněk Nehoda, which came from a corner on the stroke of half-time, was a sucker punch, though worse was yet to come. Just two minutes into the second period, Dušan Galis put the home side ahead with a powerful diving header that Clemence had little chance of saving.

Czechoslovakia disrupted England with a series of ugly challenges, and it could be argued that Revie should have realised a rough encounter was likely and factored this into the equation when he named his team. One of the Czechoslovaks, in fact, was sent off, though the player in question did not play a second of the game: after excessively remonstrating with the referee over a decision, Alexander Vencel, the substitute goalkeeper, was given his marching orders. Revie did react to the opposition's aggressive style during the game, bringing on the combative Watson, but England remained second best and succumbed to a 2-1 defeat. The result was nothing short of disastrous.

England would go into their final game of the group knowing their nearest rivals, Czechoslovakia, were playing minnows Cyprus. The gamble in Bratislava had backfired. Revie, though, said of his players, 'They did everything I wanted them to do, but there was that one vital moment when they went to sleep for a corner. No one was in the right position at the right time, and that cost us the goal which probably decided the game. I was more disappointed with the way we played when we beat Switzerland last month than in this game. And certainly I still think we can qualify for the final stages of the European Championship but, of course, it is now going to be very much more difficult. I would pick exactly the same side if I had a second chance.'

So England's fate would be decided on 19 November in Lisbon. Portugal were by no means a poor side, though they were nowhere near the team they would become in the 2000s and beyond. The retirement of their talisman Eusébio had left a gulf in their attack, and their top scorer in the European Championship qualifying campaign going into their final match was Benfica forward Nené who had netted just twice. Revie went for a more balanced team than the one that had played against Czechoslovakia. The biggest name to be dropped was Colin Bell; the Manchester City legend would never play for England again. Full-backs Whitworth and Beattie, who did not start the previous game despite strong showings against the Scots and the Swiss, both returned.

When Nené was bundled over nearly 30 yards from goal a quarter of an hour into the game, there did not appear to be much cause for concern as Portugal had committed few men forward. Rui Rodrigues, however, chose to shoot at goal from the free kick and his strike was phenomenal: Clemence dived at full stretch, but the ball met the top-right corner of the net and England found themselves behind. Their qualifying hopes almost suffered another blow when Toni dragged his shot wide – but there was a bigger scare to come. Making a surging run forward, Nené left the England defence in his tracks and attempted to chip Clemence but missed the target.

Shortly before half-time, Portugal gave away a foul just outside their penalty area. Channon's shot glanced off the wall and, although keeper Vítor Damas was not entirely deceived by the deflection, England had their equaliser. The goal should have lifted England's spirits and given them the confidence to push on. The Portuguese, however, continued to create chances and Revie's men were extremely fortunate to not end up on the wrong end of a hammering. Again Nené was guilty of missing a wonderful opportunity while João Alves also forced Clemence into action. The 1-1 draw in Lisbon meant that England temporarily went top of their group, though they would be knocked from the summit four days later when Czechoslovakia duly won 3-0 against Cyprus. England had been eliminated with a whimper.

The fallout, however, began in the immediate aftermath of the Portugal game, with Football League secretary Alan Hardaker, an arch Revie critic, unleashing an astonishing attack on the England manager. Revie had complained about the amateurish attitude of the English game and the impact that had at international level. Hardaker was having none of it and said, 'I'm a cynical man and it sounded to me that we smacked of excuses before we even left for Portugal. We have to face up to the fact that we were not good enough. It's Revie's approach to administration that is amateurish.' Revie responded, 'This is one of the biggest shocks I've had in my life. It's hard to believe that a person in such a responsible position in football should say such things. It's hurt me a little bit, but I have no wish to get into a slanging match over this, especially as it might harm England's chances in the future.'

Of the six games they had played in their group, England had only won three, and two of those victories had come against Cyprus. Displays away from home had been poor and the constant tinkering with the squads had not paid dividends. Furthermore, Revie had made his job even more difficult by upsetting influential and popular players, some of whom would go on to become his most ardent critics. There were sources of comfort for him, such as the fact that his defence had, overall, performed well having only conceded three goals in the qualifying group, though there was no hiding from what was a disastrous end to the year. Within the space of six months, Revie had experienced the elation of beating Scotland 5-1 and the misery of failing to reach the 1976 European Championship.

10

Supermac's Famous Five

THE WEMBLEY scoreboard screamed 'Supermac 5 Cyprus 0' on the night Malcolm Macdonald made history for England. The Newcastle United striker's nap hand of goals in a European Championship qualifier on 16 April 1975 saw him become the only England player to achieve the feat at the national stadium.

Macdonald was also the first player to score five goals in a game for England since Willie Hall, whose hat-trick came in the space of a mere three minutes in a 7-0 slaughter of Ireland at Old Trafford in November 1938. Four of Macdonald's goals were headers, but little was he to know that his heroics would be shunned to the extent that it would be the last time he played for England at Wembley.

In early 1975, there was a clamour among fans and the media for a 25-year-old Macdonald to receive an England recall. By the end of February, he had 27 goals that season in all competitions for his club. In his previous seven England appearances, the first of which was under Sir Alf Ramsey against Wales in 1972, he had failed to open his goal account. But after making two of those appearances as a substitute against Scotland and Yugoslavia in May and June of 1974, with Joe Mercer as caretaker boss, Macdonald's time finally came again the following March in Don Revie's third game in charge. World Cup winners West Germany were the visitors to mark the 100th international match at Wembley, and England inflicted their first defeat as world champions. Macdonald vividly remembers Revie's extraordinary greeting as he reported for duty. He said, 'I'd sort of been somewhat of a regular for a couple of seasons with Sir Alf Ramsey, a regular in the squad that is, not so much in the team. When Alf left, Joe Mercer was there for a short while and then they appointed Don Revie. He left me out of the squad for his first two games and he was struggling a bit for goals.

'He called me in for his third game and I arrived at the team hotel on the Sunday night and went and found him in the lounge with his entourage – he always had this entourage around him. I said, "Malcolm Macdonald reporting, no injuries from the game yesterday." And he just looked at me and said, "I don't want you here, I feel you've been foisted upon me by the press, so if you don't score on Wednesday, I'll never pick you again." I thought, "Woah, that's a bit strong." It wasn't quite what I expected.

'But I'm always one to look on the bright side of life and I thought, "Well, at least I know I'm playing!" West Germany had won the World Cup in 1974, but Colin Bell scored and then I scored from a great cross by Alan Ball and made it 2-0. Revie came into the dressing room after that game and he went round shaking everybody's hand and said, "Well played." He shook hands with Mick Channon next to me and walked straight past me, completely ignored me, and shook hands with the number ten and 11 – and walked out of the dressing room.

'It was a bit surprising, but I was in the squad for the Cyprus game. I arrived at the hotel, reporting again that I had no injuries from the day before, and he said, "The same applies as last time, if you don't score, I'll never pick you again." So I set my stall out just to score as many as I could that night – and finished up getting five. Nobody had ever done it at Wembley before and I was the only goalscorer on the night.'

The first of what could easily have been seven goals for Macdonald came after around only 90 seconds, a firm header from a left-wing free kick by Alan Hudson. Macdonald's pace and strength, as well as his finishing touch, had the Cypriots all at sea and when he burst down the left and centred, he almost set up a goal for Mick Channon, whose effort brushed off keeper Makis Alkiviades and cleared the crossbar. Macdonald then missed a chance with only Alkiviades to beat, but he made amends in the 32nd minute. Kevin Keegan pulled the ball back from the left and Macdonald scored with a mis-hit shot. He also struck a post with a shot with his weaker right foot, but in the second half he scored twice in four minutes, first for his hat-trick in the 52nd with a stooping header after Keegan nodded the ball back in from the left, and then from a tremendous header on the end of a right-wing cross by Dave Thomas, the winger having come off the bench moments earlier.

Left-back Kevin Beattie had a goal disallowed for a foul on Alkiviades, who as a result was forced off through injury on the hour. It meant that Macdonald's fifth goal, three minutes from time, came against a different keeper, with substitute Andreas Konstantinou being beaten by a simple, close-range header from another right-sided centre courtesy of Thomas.

Macdonald had flashed a message to Revie in the most emphatic manner imaginable, and the scoreboard operators illuminated it in spectacular style. Macdonald said, 'At the end of the game we started shaking hands with the Cypriots, and I looked up and above the tunnel at the far end of the ground, there was an electronic scoreboard that had been

121

keeping tally with the score – and it went blank. I carried on shaking hands and then it relit and I looked and this time it said, "Congratulations: Supermac 5 Cyprus 0."

'As a lad, I'd seen the England-Uruguay game that kicked off the 1966 World Cup finals and I just thought, "Wow, I'd dreamed of it then and it's actually happened now." When that scoreline was up there, reality struck and I started looking around the track from the dugouts and there was Revie in his trench coat, stooped and marching around the track towards the tunnel. And from the far end of the pitch, I screamed, pointing up at that scoreboard, "Read that and weep you bastard." Then, when we were in the dressing room, he shook hands with the goalkeeper, right-back, left-back, all the way round to Mick Channon and then completely blanked me and never said a word. And I never played at Wembley again for England.

'All I can do is make my own assumptions and what I believe is, at the time Leeds were one of the top sides in the country when I was playing for Newcastle. It was Leeds, Liverpool and Arsenal. It just seemed that I had this habit of scoring against Leeds in really tight, crucial games when they needed the points and Newcastle, with my goals, beat Leeds most times when we were at home. He quite possibly bore a grudge because of that. Otherwise, we had no other dealings prior to me joining up with the England squad with him as manager so I can only assume that he didn't like me for the goals that I'd scored that had cost Leeds dearly.'

Macdonald experienced many of Revie's quirks and found his constant tinkering with the England team odd given the loyalty he had shown to his players at Leeds. But he was all too aware that Revie also had his favourites in the England ranks, and one in particular who had no connection whatsoever with his Elland Road days. He said, 'It was strange the way he chopped and changed the team and discarded players, particularly when you consider the patience he had with players as Leeds manager and that he nurtured them and brought them through and gave them time to settle in.

'They were a formidable side and he was like a second father to them and he treated them with all the love and care that you would bestow on sons. And what I found in the England squad was that he certainly had his favourites – and he didn't mind showing it. QPR's Gerry Francis, for one. He thought the sun shone out of Gerry Francis's backside, he really did. Gerry Francis could do no wrong. Others who had played equally well, he criticised and in my case, just totally ignored. He was a man who was stringent in ways that were unnecessary. For example, he decreed that we had to wear these very thick, woolly polo-neck jumpers in training underneath our tracksuit tops.

'And the one that I got, it was so small for heaven's sake that it was very difficult to actually move freely in, and I said, "I don't want to wear this. I go through the coldest of winters in Newcastle and I've never worn a jumper yet." A shirt and a tracksuit was the most I had ever worn. "No, no, no," he said, "you have to wear the jumper." It was all silly things like that, whereas Alf, he was just absolutely full of respect for each and every individual who was there. He wanted them to feel comfortable and relaxed in the environment leading up to a match, but with Don Revie it was, "You live by my rules." If you didn't, he didn't want you there.'

On the back of his five-star show for England, however, Macdonald soon enhanced his profile even more when he appeared on the TV series *Superstars*, screened by the BBC, in which elite sportsmen battled it out in a multi-discipline competition. Football fans and defenders were already well aware of Macdonald's blistering pace, but a wider audience were amazed to see him win the 100m in an Olympic qualifying time of 10.9 seconds. Afterwards, programme presenter and commentator Ron Pickering told Macdonald that he had recorded the second-fastest time in Europe at that point in 1975. England colleagues such as Bobby Moore, Colin Bell, Stan Bowles, Channon and Keegan – who memorably came a cropper in the cycling when he suffered cuts and abrasions to his back, shoulder and arm but refused to withdraw and was the overall winner of the heat – were also among those who took part in the series.

Ultimately, however, Revie did not want Macdonald around the England scene and, if their relationship had been uneasy, the same could be said for that of the striker and his new manager at Newcastle, Gordon Lee. The goals kept coming for Macdonald in a black and white shirt and he helped the Magpies to a 1976 League Cup Final defeat by Manchester City, but Lee incurred the wrath of the Geordie fans when he agreed to sell their hero to Arsenal in a £333,333 deal which, in the scorching summer of that year, was red-hot news.

Although all six of his England goals – in winning only 14 caps – came in Revie's time, Macdonald was more comfortable playing under Ramsey and also warmed to Mercer, who took the job on temporarily despite a debilitating physical problem. He said, 'Bless him, he was a lovely, lovely guy, but at the time, he was suffering dreadfully, I think it was with his back. He couldn't sleep properly, he couldn't lie down on a bed. He had to spend his nights sitting propped up in a chair. You could see it was quite wearing on him.

'He was a terrific fella but he again had me sidelined, which I always found exceedingly frustrating. His attention was on the XI due to start, like most managers. Nobody had that all-embracing manner which Sir Alf managed. I thoroughly enjoyed playing under Alf and playing to his instructions. As I've said, he had huge respect for every one of his players and treated you as such.'

But Ramsey made an exception for one player who, as Macdonald remembers, tested the manager's patience to the limit. He said, 'I made my debut against Wales in Cardiff in 1972, playing alongside Rodney Marsh and Mike Summerbee, two Manchester City lads. We were the three forwards and they sort of played one-twos all the while between them and I was a bit left out of it. We lost to Northern Ireland at Wembley on the Wednesday night so it meant we had to beat Scotland to finish level at the top of the table with them and, of course, my skipper at Newcastle, Bob Moncur, played for Scotland in that game. I was a sub, England were leading 1-0 through a goal by Alan Ball in the first half. There were 120,000 drunken Scots and late in the game Rodney tried one of his tricks in the Scotland penalty area and Alf Ramsey just turned to his assistant, Harold Shepherdson, and said, "Get him off." Then he turned the other way to me and said, "Get yourself changed quickly." So I got myself ready and did a few sprints and Rodney came off – and hardly played again for England. Alf had run out of patience with him.

'And Alf kept saying to me "run the ball into the corners" and that's what I did and we finished up winning 1-0. When something happened in that game, the crowd would roar and there was this massive gust of stale beer. It wasn't what you wanted on a very sober football pitch. That was the biggest crowd I ever played in front of. It was quite something.'

11

Hitmen and Mavericks

NOT ONLY did England's struggles throughout the 1970s conflict with the nation's successes in Europe at club level, they were also in marked contrast to the vast array of talent that was at the country's disposal. It was almost as if the likes of Sir Alf Ramsey and Don Revie did not know which way to turn, notably when it came to attacking players.

Just consider how much strength in depth there was in terms of strikers or forwards alone in the English game in the first few years of the decade when running through, in no particular order, this sample list: Geoff Hurst, Francis Lee, Allan Clarke, Peter Osgood, Jeff Astle, Brian Kidd, Joe Royle, Martin Chivers, Malcolm Macdonald, Mick Jones and John Radford. That is literally a team and all of them won at least one cap in the period from 1970 to 1972. Manchester United's Kidd, a member of their European Cup-winning side in 1968, was the unlucky one ahead of the Mexico World Cup when he failed to make the cut for Ramsey's final squad despite scoring as a substitute in the game that preceded the tournament, a 2-0 warm-up win in Ecuador.

In Mexico, West Ham's Hurst and Manchester City's Lee were Ramsey's preferred front two, though he rested them for the final group game against Czechoslovakia, opting for West

Brom's Astle and Clarke of Leeds, with Chelsea's Osgood making his second substitute appearance of the tournament. Osgood is good was the mantra down Kings Road where 'Ossie' was an idol, but he was kept waiting another three and a half years for his next England cap – and the last of just four – in a 1-0 defeat by Italy at Wembley.

Hurst and Clarke were the only England frontmen to score in Mexico, the former in the opening group match with Romania and the latter, with a penalty, against the Czechoslovaks in the 1-0 victories that came either side of the solitary-goal defeat by Brazil. The form of Chivers for Tottenham made him a beneficiary of the fallout from England's failure to defend the World Cup and he seized his chance with five goals in as many games at the start of his international career. Yet he suffered, as did many, after a place at the 1974 tournament slipped through England's fingers, and a deterioration in form for his club hardly helped his prospects, with his relationship with legendary 1961 double-winning manager, Bill Nicholson, becoming strained.

After scoring 13 goals in 24 appearances in a little over two and a half years on the international stage, Chivers's England days came to an abrupt end when he was substituted and Derby's Kevin Hector was thrown on in his place in the traumatic 1-1 draw with Poland at Wembley in October 1973 as hopes of World Cup qualification were obliterated. Kevin Keegan, who was also on the bench that night, tells a story that he thought it was he – not the other Kevin – who had been ordered to prepare to go on and was beginning to do so, with Ray Clemence unhelpfully pulling his shorts down in the scramble to discard his tracksuit bottoms, when he realised the call was for Hector to win the first of only two caps, both coming as a substitute.

But England were blessed with many more versatile forward players in those years and beyond: Keegan, and his big friend in football and horse racing, Mick Channon, and Mike Summerbee being good examples. Macdonald, always remembered by England fans for his five goals against Cyprus at Wembley in 1975, readily acknowledges that he operated in a golden age for strikers. He said, 'I played for England in a period of a bit less than four years and, very quickly, I counted as many forwards as I could who had been in the England squad around that time. I reckon I got to 26! I knew there were others I'd probably forgotten and others who didn't even get in – like Pop Robson. Many, many years later, I made this known on the radio programme I did and said, "Now, I would like you to name ten current England forwards." And no one could do it. They came up with six!' The likes of Ipswich and Liverpool striker David Johnson, Manchester United's Stuart Pearson, Ipswich's Paul Mariner, Everton's Bob Latchford and Nottingham Forest's Tony Woodcock all appeared for England's senior side in the late 1970s and, in the case of some, beyond.

A breed of flashier forwards with flair also made their names in the decade, and one of the factors in it being such a fallow period for England was perhaps a fundamental failure to fully harness and make the most of the abilities of more of them in the international setup. The definition of a maverick is someone independent or unorthodox, and in this era English football had more than its fair share of that ilk. The freedom of expression, as many in the game call it, has been restrained to some extent over the years by a greater emphasis on tactics, systems and more disciplined defending. It can be argued that it has come at a cost in terms of individuality.

Rodney Marsh, a swaggering striker with extravagant skills, was one of several England players in the 1970s for whom the word maverick could have been invented. Long-haired and with a rebellious streak to match, the highly opinionated Marsh demonstrated precious little deference and that inclination was surely one of the reasons why he won just nine England caps. A pre-match comment to manager Ramsey was characteristic and telling. As Marsh himself recalled, Ramsey said, 'If you don't work hard I'm going to pull you off at half-time.' Marsh responded, 'Crikey, at Manchester City all we get is a cup of tea and an orange.' That type of levity was alien to Ramsey – and it was the last time Marsh played for England. Fulham was the launch pad for his career, where he learned from the great England inside-forward Johnny Haynes. It was with Queens Park Rangers, though, that his talent flourished as he played his part in successive promotions, which took them from the Third Division to the top flight, and the 1967 League Cup Final win against First Division West Brom at Wembley, where Marsh scored a superlative individual goal.

Manchester City boss Malcolm Allison, who had taken over team affairs from Joe Mercer at Maine Road, was impressed enough with Marsh to persuade his predecessor, by then general manager, and the board to pay a club-record £200,000 for the forward in March 1972. Yet his time with City divides opinion, many believing Marsh's arrival upset the applecart and cost the club the league title that season. City were sitting pretty at the top of the table when Marsh signed, but his languid, ball-playing style slowed the tempo of their game. Brian Clough's Derby snatched the title, City dropping to fourth but finishing only a point behind the champions. In the twilight of his playing days, Marsh made a memorable return to Fulham on loan from United States side Tampa Bay Rowdies, and played in a typically cavalier fashion in tandem with his pal George Best at Craven Cottage.

Stan Bowles was almost a mirror image of Marsh, whose mantle he assumed at QPR. That came in the slipstream of Marsh's move to City – who just happened to be Bowles's first club. Bowles had done himself no favours at Maine Road by clashing with another big persona in coach Allison, and he drifted from Bury to Crewe Alexandra and Carlisle United before QPR gave him a stage for his showmanship. The parallels between Marsh and Bowles were uncanny. When Bowles scored his only England goal in his five appearances in a win against Wales at Ninian Park in 1974, it was two years after Marsh's sole strike for his country in a victory at the same ground.

A mischievous Bowles seemed to take pleasure in antagonising the opposition. After Sunderland had won the FA Cup with their shock victory over Revie's Leeds at Wembley in 1973, the Wearsiders paraded the trophy ahead of a game against QPR at Roker Park four days later.

The cup was placed on a pitchside table and in the warm-up Bowles bet with a team-mate on who could fire a shot at the silverware and knock it off its pedestal. When the feat was performed during the game, it provoked an angry reaction from the home fans. Some invaded the pitch after Micky Horswill's sending-off for retaliating to a Bowles challenge, forcing the match to be halted and Sunderland boss Bob Stokoe to appeal for calm on a microphone. The fact QPR won 3-0, Bowles scoring twice, didn't help the mood.

Bowles was controversial, but his adroit flamboyance ensured he became a QPR legend. One well-worn anecdote was that if you rolled up at Loftus Road shortly before kick-off, you might bump into Stan the Man coming out of the nearest betting shop. Petulance often got the better of him. In an FA Cup fifth-round tie at West Ham in February 1975, QPR boss Dave Sexton substituted Bowles, who gestured angrily and mouthed at his manager as he left the field. He later vowed he would never speak to Sexton again.

But that was Bowles all over. The next season, he helped to inspire QPR's title challenge, scoring ten times in the league as Liverpool – with Keegan among the goals at Molineux – pipped them by a point with a 3-1 win over Wolves after Sexton's side had led the table for much of the closing weeks of the campaign. The legendary Wolves forward Derek Dougan, something of a maverick himself, felt that Revie was wrong to recall Bowles to the England side in November 1976, after a two-and-a-half-year absence, for the World Cup qualifier with Italy in Rome, which ended in a 2-0 defeat. 'The Doog', as the outspoken Northern Ireland star was dubbed, said Revie ought to have stuck with Manchester City winger Dennis Tueart, who had scored along with club-mate Royle in the 2-1 home win over Finland a month earlier.

Bowles's hair-trigger temper had also famously flared when he walked out on England after being substituted in a 1-0 win against Northern Ireland at Wembley in May 1974. His international exile followed and he made only two more appearances for his country. Tommy Docherty's return as QPR boss heralded the end of Bowles's time with the club. The pair did not see eye-to-eye and relations were no better with a certain Mr Clough, who paid £210,000 to take Bowles to Forest in December 1979. Even Clough failed to tame him, though with two such strong personalities involved it was no surprise that their relationship was fractious. When Bowles effectively ruled himself out of Forest's 1980 European Cup Final against Keegan's Hamburg, after Clough had refused to let him play in big friend John Robertson's testimonial match, the writing was on the wall. That summer, after only six months or so at the City Ground, Bowles was on his way back to London where he joined Orient.

It was somehow appropriate that when he was withdrawn by Mercer against Northern Ireland, it marked an England debut for another maverick, his replacement Frank Worthington, who was then with Leicester. Ian Greaves, his manager at Huddersfield early in his career, labelled

Worthington 'the working man's George Best'. A striker blessed with an intrinsic touch, 'Worthy' was a wonderful crowd-pleaser. Although it was late in his playing days and into the early years of the 1980s, the Sunderland fans who Bowles had tormented were among those lucky enough to see Worthington in their colours, as were followers of Bolton, Birmingham, Leeds, Southampton and more in a nomadic career. What would have been the biggest move of his career, from Huddersfield to Liverpool in 1972, fell through, however. He was pictured signing on the dotted line, with Reds manager Bill Shankly and his assistant, Bob Paisley, looking over Worthington's shoulder, but failed a medical – twice – due to high blood pressure, which he later attributed to his self-indulgent social life.

Both on and off the pitch, Worthington had a distinct style, but the casual wear he sported did not win the approval of the austere Ramsey when he reputedly arrived at Heathrow Airport in cowboy boots, a red silk shirt and a lime-green velvet jacket. Worthington likened himself to a peacock and he certainly liked to strut his stuff. He worshipped Elvis Presley, 'The King of Rock 'n' Roll'. Worthington was often 'The King' on the football field and he rocked and rolled a good many opponents, but he failed to reign as an England player with two goals in only eight games.

Charlie George was another with long locks and loads of dash. He will always be remembered for his outstanding FA Cup Final-winning goal for Arsenal against Liverpool in 1971. A thunderous, long-range shot, followed by a flat-out, arms-outstretched celebration, clinched a first double for the Gunners. Injuries didn't help George and he left for Derby in 1975, scoring a hat-trick against Real Madrid in the European Cup. It was with the Rams that he won his only England cap in a 1-1 friendly draw with the Republic of Ireland at Wembley in 1976. In terms of the high profile he enjoyed in the domestic game, if ever there was a 'One-Cap Wonder', it was George, a forward whose talent was unfulfilled. Like Bowles, George experienced life under Clough, but despite scoring the only goal in the home leg of Forest's European Super Cup Final win over Barcelona in January 1980, an extension to his short-term loan from Southampton could not be agreed.

Tony Currie was nowhere near as outlandish as some of the aforementioned, but he was still something of an outlier and started for the England side infamously held by Poland in 1973. The Sheffield United legend, who went on to play for Leeds and QPR, was an attack-minded midfielder who thrived on a free role but often played wide. Few who were around in the 1970s could forget his fabulous stroll through a bewitched West Ham defence to roll the ball into the net in the most nonchalant manner for his beloved Blades at Bramall Lane. It was Currie at his hottest, but he won only 17 caps.

Alan Hudson was a player with abundant ability in his days with Chelsea and Stoke City. When still a teenager, the midfielder was in contention for a place in the 1970 World Cup squad among the 12-strong group of reserves. Having played in every round of Chelsea's run to their FA Cup Final with Leeds, Hudson then missed the trip to Wembley and the replay, the victim of an ankle injury. It put paid to any hope he had of making it to Mexico and, astonishingly, he had to wait nearly another five years before he won his first senior England cap, in a 2-0 Wembley win against West Germany. By then, Hudson – one of the so-called 'Kings Road Playboys' and born and bred close to that fashionable stretch of west London – had left the bright lights behind for Stoke in a £240,000 deal that was, at the time, a British transfer record.

A month after his first England appearance, he made his second and what was to be his last for his country in the Macdonald match against Cyprus. In the main, Hudson's was a career that fell well short of its potential – certainly at international level – and in 1997 he suffered devastating injuries when he was hit by a car. Such was his dissatisfaction with his England career and the FA that, in 2021, he revealed in an interview with the *Daily Mail* that he had written to English football's governing body, insisting his meagre statistics for his country should be expunged from the record.

It was notable that it was players seen to have more of a work ethic, a willingness and an ability to fit into a team pattern, the likes of Keegan and Trevor Francis – Britain's first £1m footballer when Clough signed him for Forest from Birmingham City in 1979 – and dependable Chelsea and Manchester United midfielder Ray Wilkins, who enjoyed greater longevity in England colours than the often-maddening but much-admired mavericks. Keegan debuted for England in 1972 and won 63 caps in his ten years as an international player, Francis picked up 52 from 1977 to 1986, and Wilkins garnered 84 in a decade on the scene for the Three Lions, the first coming in 1976.

12

'Finnish' Line Looms

EIGHT DAYS before England's first game of 1976, prime minister Harold Wilson announced his resignation; there were many people in the country who wished Don Revie would do likewise. Unseeded going into the draw to determine their World Cup qualifying group, England had already discovered that they would need to better Italy in order to return to international football's foremost competition two years hence. Going on the *Azzurri*'s disappointing showing at the 1974 World Cup and the fact that England were unseeded, it appeared at that moment as though Revie's men had perhaps been given a reasonable draw as they could potentially have been placed with either the Netherlands or France. Revie told multiple sources that he was very happy with the draw, though he must have known deep down the scale of the task before him.

Wales were celebrating the centenary of their FA, and a friendly against England at the Racecourse Ground, Wrexham had been arranged to mark the occasion. No fewer than six debutants were named in the England starting line-up: Liverpool trio Phil Neal, Phil Thompson and Ray Kennedy, Leeds United's Trevor Cherry, Manchester City's Mike Doyle and Norwich City's Phil Boyer. Dave Clement, of Queens Park Rangers, also won his first cap as a substitute, although it was the other sub who provided the big story before kick-off. Winger Peter Taylor was 23 and plying his trade at Third Division Crystal Palace, and when he was brought on at half-time he became the first player since Johnny Byrne in 1961 (who was also with Palace at the time) to represent England while playing in the third tier. For the first time in his international career, Kevin Keegan was given the role of captain. Kennedy, who was an integral member of the Liverpool squad that would be crowned First Division champions that year, opened the scoring in the 70th minute. Ten minutes later, Taylor made it 2-0 before Alan Curtis of Swansea City grabbed a late consolation for Wales.

In May, England travelled back to Wales, but this time the venue was Ninian Park, Cardiff. Despite the inexperience at senior international level of the experimental side that had played at Wrexham, Revie showed a fair deal of faith by retaining the majority of the team, although there were first caps for Manchester United utility man Brian Greenhoff, his club-mate striker Stuart Pearson, and Sunderland midfielder Tony Towers. Taylor, promoted to a starting berth following his effective display in the previous match, scored the only goal of the game to continue England's unblemished start to the year.

Two narrow wins over the Welsh had neither weakened Revie's position nor strengthened it, but the match against Northern Ireland on 11 May would give the former Leeds supremo some much-needed relief. Having survived an early scare when Ray Clemence had pulled off a point-blank save to deny Bryan Hamilton, England took the lead when Gerry Francis, latching on to a backheel from Mick Channon, rounded Pat Jennings before calmly guiding the ball into the net. Only a minute later, Jennings was retrieving the ball from his goal once more: Channon was too quick for Newcastle

United's Tommy Cassidy, who gave the referee an easy decision when he blatantly scythed down the forward from behind, and Channon made no mistake from the penalty spot. In the second half, Pearson scored his maiden international goal on only his second appearance when Kennedy's shot was parried into his path before the in-form Channon completed the 4-0 rout with a cool finish.

The British Home Championship would be decided on 15 May at Hampden Park. Scotland had also secured maximum points from their two games going into the encounter, and they had, unusually, been given the opportunity to play all their matches of that year's tournament at home. The only change for England was enforced: Greenhoff had believed that an injury he had picked up was innocuous, but overnight his knee had become swollen so Derby County's Roy McFarland took his place in central defence. Hampden was, as ever, a bear-pit and the cheers of the England followers when their team took the lead could barely be heard. The move started with an excellent interception by McFarland in the centre circle. The defender took the ball forward, then, after playing a one-two with Taylor, crossed for Channon. The Southampton man expertly peeled away from his marker to nod home, but the Scots levelled almost immediately. Don Masson, who played alongside Francis at Queens Park Rangers, hit back with a fine header from a corner. England did have the ball in the net once more in the first half, though Keegan's strike was in vain as seconds before he had knocked the ball over the line the referee, Hungarian Károly Palotai, had correctly blown for a foul when Pearson had barged keeper Alan Rough while they were challenging for the same cross.

There was a moment of controversy in the later stages of the half when Kenny Dalglish made a daring run into the box and Clemence threw himself at his feet. The Scotland forward fell face down, but the referee did not point to the spot, much to the annoyance of the majority of the crowd. Replays suggested that there had been little or no contact. One of the most memorable aspects of the match was the battle between future Liverpool team-mates Clemence and Dalglish. In the second half, a poor back pass by Kennedy resulted in Dalglish clattering into Clemence as the keeper scooped up the ball. The Anfield shot-stopper was clearly in discomfort following the collision, and the effects of that coming together may have been partly to blame for what would prove to be the crucial goal. Soon afterwards, McFarland failed with an attempt to dispossess Joe Jordan with a sliding tackle ten yards into England's half and, despite the best efforts of Colin Todd to catch up with the charging Scot, Jordan delivered a cross into the box. Dalglish's first touch was superb, but although his shot was low and tame, the ball squirmed between the legs of Clemence and over the line. The BBC's David Coleman remarked, 'Clemence's day is now complete – a total disaster.' It is the nature of the game that goalkeeping mistakes are, more often than not, the most costly. But placing such emphasis on Clemence's display was perhaps a little harsh from the veteran commentator because the keeper was by no means the only England player to make an error that afternoon and he had, up until that point, been one of their best performers. Though Scotland pressed for a third, Dalglish's goal proved decisive as England lost 2-1. Revie, understandably, made a quick exit down the tunnel on the final whistle.

Following the disappointing end to the Home Championship, England jetted off to play in the USA Bicentennial Cup. Brazil, Italy, England and an all-stars team comprising players then playing in the North American Soccer League contested a four-team group. At the time, the NASL was in its heyday with hundreds of some of the most decorated players to ever grace the game eager to sign for American clubs. The first game for England was in Los Angeles against the mighty Brazil, who had been through a sobering end to 1975 when they were unceremoniously dumped out of the Copa América by eventual winners Peru.

Eight who started against Scotland kept their places with Trevor Brooking, Cherry and Doyle the only incoming players. The matchday attendance was less than half the crowd at Hampden, and those who did turn up were not treated to the most exciting exhibition. England held their own against the Brazilians for the majority of the match and appeared to be the more likely side to find a winner. There was an explosive ending in store, however, when Brazil's Roberto Dinamite came up with an archetypal poacher's finish after England had failed to clear from a corner. It was the only goal of the game.

Then-FIFA president João Havelange was in attendance when England played Italy on 28 May at Yankee Stadium, New York. Although the crowd of more than 40,000 was one of the biggest ever to watch a football match in the US, the fact that the *New York Times*, on the day of the game, only dedicated a short article on the build-up on page 16 showed that soccer – as the Americans always call it – still had some way to go to come close to rivalling the nation's dominant sports, such as American football and basketball. Revie sprang a surprise before the game by announcing that many of his stars, including Keegan, would not start. This led to the suspicion that Keegan was being protected ahead of the World Cup qualifier between the sides later in the year. Fulvio Bernardini, technical director for Italy, was far from impressed about the forward's absence. 'If Don Revie is trying to hide Keegan, then there's a double-edged sword because we will hide the defence we plan to use to stop Keegan,' he told the *Daily News*. Arsenal keeper Jimmy Rimmer was handed his one and only England cap while Chelsea midfielder Ray

Wilkins and Manchester United winger Gordon Hill were also given their debuts. The pitch was perhaps the most bizarre playing surface that either side had ever played on: though most of it was converted specially for the game, the baseball diamonds were left untouched meaning that there were large sections of sand on the field of play. To add to the peculiarity, the coaches and substitutes did not sit in the baseball dugouts and instead lined up on benches that ran along the side of the pitch in a scene more reminiscent of a schools' match than an international fixture.

England found themselves two goals behind in the opening 20 minutes; Doyle was first dispossessed after failing to control a chip from Towers, resulting in Francesco Graziani scoring on the break, and the Italian forward then doubled his tally thanks to some poor marking from the England back line. Revie changed goalkeepers at half-time with Rimmer making way for debutant Joe Corrigan in a move that had already been arranged before the game. Having been fortunate not to be further behind at the restart, England stunned Italy with quick-fire goals from Channon and Thompson. With the momentum in their favour, England then took the lead when Channon, the captain for the day in the absence of Gerry Francis, placed the ball through the legs of Dino Zoff. The remarkable turnaround came in the space of just eight minutes. There was late drama when Giacinto Facchetti believed he had scored an equaliser deep into added time, though the goal did not stand as the referee spotted that Fabio Capello had shoved Corrigan in the build-up. The manner of the 3-2 victory and the fact that the Italians had fielded a near full-strength side instilled plenty of hope that England could beat them in the World Cup qualifiers. Revie was understandably pleased with the result when he was interviewed after the game. He told ITV, 'I thought we played reasonably well, but the Italians looked really good,

I must admit, the first half hour and they possibly deserved their two-goal lead. But this game, one minute you're up and one minute you're down – Sunday night we were down because we lost against Brazil and tonight we're a bit more pleased. But what a set of characters.'

Their third and final game of the tour was in Pennsylvania three days later against the NASL all-stars team. Two former England internationals in Tommy Smith (who was on loan at Tampa Bay Rowdies at the time from Liverpool) and none other than Bobby Moore would line up alongside Northern Ireland's Dave Clements, Mike England of Wales and all-time great Pelé. Despite the fact that there were only a handful of American internationals in the team, they were given the name 'Team America'. For obvious reasons, the game was not classed as an official match by FIFA, though this did not deter Revie from recalling many of his key players to the side. It did not take long for England to seize control. Keegan scored first after being teed up by Brooking from a free kick and then with a placed finish. A classy goal from Francis, in which he took the ball past the opposition keeper before scoring into an empty net, ended the match as a contest; however, Team America did pull a late goal back, ex-Watford and Sheffield United winger Stewart Scullion scoring his side's only goal of the tournament. Though the performances had been generally positive, it is unlikely much was learned from England's tour of the United States, and many of those on the periphery, who had been given opportunities to impress, did not play in any of the year's remaining games.

Revie picked an experienced side to begin the World Cup qualifying campaign with only three of those he named in the starting line-up holding fewer than 12 caps. Finland had never beaten England at senior level before, and even the most pessimistic of Three Lions fans believed the result would be a foregone conclusion. However, knowing from the outset that they were in a two-way fight with the Italians, it was clear that goal difference could play a major role in deciding who progressed to the finals, meaning achieving big wins home and away against Finland and Luxembourg was imperative for England. Revie summed up the weight of expectation, saying, 'This is the most important match I have faced in my 15 years as a manager. Qualifying for the World Cup finals is more difficult than what you face when you get there; Poland proved that in 1974. They could have been beaten 6-0 by England but once they reached the finals, they improved with every match.'

But Revie was in confident mood and traced a togetherness in his squad back to the Welsh centenary game. He said, 'Things have started to fall into place fairly quickly since then. Players came into the side who wanted to play for England and didn't mind travelling. Having the squad together for five or six weeks since the British Championship has also helped.' Revie hoped his side would 'play as well as we did against Brazil and put two or three chances in the back of the net'. Pearson obliged when he struck early on, but Finland pegged England back through a goal from Matti Paatelainen, father of future Bolton Wanderers striker Mixu. The setback was only temporary, and a goal from Keegan restored the lead just three minutes later. The Finns managed to carve out further chances for themselves, but a goal from Channon and Keegan's second of the game gave England a thoroughly deserved 4-1 win in Helsinki.

The match had been played the same month that Revie had received some bad news: Sir Harold Thompson had succeeded Sir Andrew Stephen as chairman of the FA. As he had been one of the most powerful men in the FA since the 1960s, it was no surprise to anyone that Thompson had ascended to the position of chairman, though for Revie it did make his job even more difficult. Thompson, an autocrat who had been a professor of chemistry at Oxford University, where one of his students was future prime minister Margaret Thatcher, was known for his unfortunate manner, especially in his handling of people he deemed to be beneath him, and on more than one occasion he derided Revie when speaking to him in public. Over time, Thompson would become one of Revie's greatest enemies, and their grudge would last until Thompson's death in 1983.

A friendly against the Republic of Ireland was arranged as a warm-up match for the second clash against Finland. Wembley was just over half-capacity on the night and the game would not go down as a classic. Pearson gave England the lead with a volley before Wilkins conceded a penalty which Gerry Daly converted for the Irish. An England side that included only two players with an international goal to their name struggled to take control of the match, and the scores remained level at the final whistle. The most notable aspect was that Charlie George made his one and only England appearance. George, who was at Derby at the time, arguably played the best football of his career earlier in the decade while with Arsenal. Although he was involved in the build-up to Pearson's goal, the attacker did not have a good game by his standards, and Revie substituted him after an hour.

The expectations were on England to brush aside a Finland team that contained many part-timers at Wembley. A young defence was chosen for the game with Todd the oldest player of the back line at just 27. Playing with a 4-2-4 formation, England's attack overwhelmed the Finns within the first three minutes. After a scramble in the box in which Joe Royle saw an attempt cleared off the line by a handball from Finnish defender Esko Ranta, Dennis Tueart fired home his first England goal. England failed to capitalise on their early dominance, and Finland had a wonderful opportunity to pull level when Jyrki Nieminen made a surging run from the halfway line which led to Clemence choosing to charge out of his box to close down the Finnish number nine. In a later era, the England keeper would have received a straight red card for his body-check on Nieminen, but the rules of the time meant that Clemence was not given his marching orders despite the fact that he had quite obviously denied his opponent a goalscoring opportunity. The resultant free kick came to nothing, and England trudged off at half-time with a slender lead. Revie's team talk appeared to do little to galvanise his side after the restart while Finland picked up where they had left off with some slick play. Minutes into the half, Aki Heiskanen approached England's box unopposed before feeding the ball to Nieminen who brought the scores level with a low finish. Clemence was partially at fault as there was not a great deal of power behind the shot, though it was the ease with which the Finns had cut through the England defence that was embarrassing.

Regaining some composure, England were able to retake the lead courtesy of a close-range header from Royle. Though they did manage to get the ball in the Finnish net once more – Kevin Beattie's effort was chalked off for offside – England had to settle for what was a bitterly disappointing 2-1 win. The crowd, having watched their team struggle against a side that included a PE teacher, an accountant and a fireman, made their displeasure known at the final whistle with a chorus of boos. It was a very understandable reaction considering just a month earlier the Finns had been decimated 6-0 in a friendly against Scotland at Hampden Park.

The poor performance against Finland would, however, have been all but forgotten if England had beaten Italy on 17 November. Revie took the bold move of dismantling his defence for the game with Greenhoff the sole defender to retain his place in the starting line-up, while there was a recall for the mercurial talent of Stan Bowles in attack. The biggest story of the squad announcement came with the return of Emlyn Hughes, who had not played for England since May the previous year.

The teams were evenly matched in the first half an hour, but a free kick from Giancarlo Antognoni, which took a wicked deflection off Keegan, gave the Italians the lead. A well-drilled Italy limited England to only a handful of chances, Greenhoff ballooning one of his team's few opportunities over the bar from just outside the six-yard box. England steadily grew into the game, but 13 minutes from time a practically unmarked Roberto Bettega headed home Italy's second. Channon later told the *Daily Star*, 'That game in 1976 was torture. They murdered us and we never got over it. It was baking hot and the pitch was so hard it was like a road. They man-marked so tightly you would have found no room pinned up against a wall. I was marked by their captain, Giacinto Facchetti, and although it was his last game for Italy, he was still ruthless.' Revie pulled no punches in his post-match reaction, saying, 'Our fate is now in other people's hands. We have to rely on Finland and Luxembourg to upset the Italians. I am naturally disappointed. The goals came at a crucial time, especially the first.'

Halfway into their qualifying campaign, England faced an uphill battle. It was near inconceivable that Italy would drop points against Finland or Luxembourg, which meant England had to not only beat them at Wembley, but also better their goal difference. With few allies among the FA hierarchy and a barrage of criticism from the fans, the writing was perhaps already on the wall for Revie that he would not be manager of England for much longer. There were not many people in the country, however, who could have predicted the events of the following year.

13

Home Truths

ENGLAND EMBARKED on a tour of South America in the summer of 1977, hoping that they would be returning for the World Cup in Argentina a year later. But Don Revie's regime was already unravelling, with a poor start to qualifying and a dismal British Home Championship, which was notable for two defeats at Wembley in five days – and the second one in particular. Those setbacks took England's losses under the Twin Towers to three in total in the calendar year, beginning with a 2-0 home defeat by the Netherlands, in which burgeoning Birmingham City forward Trevor Francis made his much-predicted debut.

England were outclassed by a Dutch side captained by the great Johan Cruyff and also featuring the likes of Johan Neeskens, Ruud Krol and Johnny Rep. It was, as the game of the Dutch was dubbed, 'Total Football' – and total dominance. Many observers regarded it as England's most comprehensive home defeat since Hungary's historic 6-3 victory at Wembley 24 years earlier. But amid the galaxy of stars on display it was a rookie, winger Jan Peters, in only his second game for the Netherlands, who shone as brightly as any with quick-fire goals in the 30th and 37th minutes to leave England deflated. The home side had hardly helped themselves, though, by playing with ten men when the Dutch scored their second goal as they delayed replacing the injured Brian Greenhoff with Colin Todd. Francis said, 'I had waited a long time to make my international debut and was thrilled when Don Revie chose me to play. It wasn't the greatest of starts for me, but I know I won't be alone when I say it was no disgrace on this particular occasion because that Dutch team contained some very special players.'

A level of home pride was restored in the following month with a 5-0 thrashing of Luxembourg at Wembley in a World Cup qualifier, Francis scoring his first England goal and Kevin Keegan, Ray Kennedy and a Mick Channon double dispatching the minnows. Keegan headed in from close range in the 11th minute after Dave Watson had lifted the ball across the box, but England had to wait until close to the hour for a second strike. Watson looped a header towards goal and Keegan and Gordon Hill went for the same ball, with the Manchester United winger nodding down for Francis to rush in and finish left-footed.

Kennedy was foiled by a goal-line clearance and Channon should have been awarded a penalty after being brought to the ground. Francis then centred and Channon challenged in the air before the ball broke kindly for Kennedy, who this time found a way through as his shot just scraped in at the near post with 65 minutes gone. It was rapid-fire at last from England as Channon's bullet header four minutes later had the pace taken off it but still managed to bobble just over the line to make it 4-0. Channon also won and slotted home a spot kick after 81 minutes to atone for his earlier denial after being generously adjudged to have been upended by Luxembourg skipper Louis Pilot. The game, which ended with the visitors down to ten men after the late dismissal of Gilbert Dresch for a second bookable offence, saw Ipswich striker Paul Mariner come off the bench to win his first cap, while John Gidman's arrival on the senior international scene drew an enormous compliment from Revie, who described the Aston Villa right-back's debut as the best England bow since the great Duncan Edwards of Manchester United 22 years earlier.

As good as Gidman was, it was still a surprising assessment by Revie given that, had Dave Clement of Queens Park Rangers not been ruled out through injury, the Liverpudlian may not have been selected. In retrospect, Revie's statement was staggering because, not only was it Gidman's first appearance for England – it was his last.

When England began the Home Championship with a 2-1 win against Northern Ireland in Belfast, Revie had revamped his side again, with Mariner making his first start for his country and midfielder Brian Talbot picking up a maiden cap as a second-half substitute who was to have an impressive impact. Mariner had been in Revie's thoughts for some time, with the manager having admitted that he was immediately impressed by the former Plymouth player when he made his debut for Bobby Robson's Ipswich in a 1-0 win at Manchester United in October 1976. Revie was especially taken with Mariner's ability on the ball for a centre-forward as well as the threat he posed in the air.

But England were forced to come from behind against the Irish after Chris McGrath, who had spent the season in Manchester United's reserves, gave his spirited side a fourth-minute lead. Dave Watson unfamiliarly failed to deal with the ball in the penalty area and Gerry Armstrong fashioned a shot which Peter Shilton could only push out to the unmarked McGrath, who tapped into an unguarded goal. It took a barnstorming break from Todd to bring England back into the game in the 27th minute when he played the perfect ball for Channon to lift his finish beyond Pat Jennings, who had dived at his feet.

England, however, had to wait until four minutes from the end for their winner, courtesy of Dennis Tueart's superb diving header from Talbot's right-wing cross. While England had spurned some chances throughout the match, they were fortunate to come away with a victory after withstanding a considerable amount of Irish pressure which was renewed after Tueart's goal and almost produced an equaliser for McGrath, who forced a flying save from Shilton with a crisply struck half-volley.

If that performance was hardly convincing, Wales further exposed England's frailties with their first Wembley win – at the 13th attempt. That it should finally arrive in Her Majesty The Queen's Silver Jubilee year was somehow appropriate, given that Wales' first Wembley visit had been in 1952, the year she came to the throne. England were sloppy from the start and the Welsh were, as ever, fired up for the occasion. Terry Yorath, one of Revie's band of brothers at Leeds, was booked for a late challenge on Greenhoff, who found himself in the wars again after being injured against the Dutch. England should have been punished by Peter Sayer, who planted a free header wide, but Wales still established a lead shortly before half-time. Shilton brought down winger Leighton James after a misunderstanding between the keeper and Emlyn Hughes. For all the outstanding saves Shilton made throughout his illustrious career, he was never renowned as a saver of penalties and James ensured he was not allowed to enhance his reputation an iota in that respect as he slotted the spot kick into the corner of the net, with the Stoke man swaying the wrong way to his left. That was to prove the difference between the sides as Wales also beat England for the first time since winning 2-1 at Cardiff in 1955, with the last victory on English territory being by the same scoreline in 1936 at Molineux.

England had lacked energy and attacking ideas and, though they exerted greater pressure and carried more threat in the second half – when hopeful penalty appeals were dismissed after striker Stuart Pearson tumbled spectacularly in colliding with keeper Dai Davies – they could not break down the red Welsh wall. That despite Revie going gung-ho with winger Tueart sent on in place of midfielder Trevor Brooking. Wales, however, did need a late, match-winning save from Davies, who splendidly pushed aside Channon's shot.

There was little time to dissect the display against Wales before Scotland, smelling blood as England licked their Wembley wounds, marched on the Twin Towers. The portents were not good for England and, for the second successive year, they suffered a 2-1 Home Championship defeat in this fixture as the rampaging Tartan Army celebrated as they had after their victory at Wembley ten years earlier.

The scenes in 1977, however, were worse – certainly from an English perspective – with the visiting fans not only tearing up the turf but also pulling down the crossbars to add to England's humiliation. Former Manchester United centre-back Gordon McQueen, then of Leeds and who played under Revie at Elland Road, etched his name in the folklore of England-Scotland rivalry. Having scored against Northern Ireland days earlier, it was McQueen's towering 43rd-minute header, on the end of Asa Hartford's neatly chipped, left-wing free kick, which handed the Scots a first-half lead. Hartford also prompted the move for Scotland's second goal as the hour mark approached, when he released tricky winger Willie Johnston on the left flank. The cross was headed back across goal by Bruce Rioch and after Kenny Dalglish's first effort was blocked, his follow-up squirmed through with the assistance of a deflection to beat Ray Clemence.

In the closing minutes, McQueen was adjudged to have brought down Trevor Francis and Channon sent Alan Rough the wrong way from the penalty spot, but it was too late to spark an England fightback. McQueen, capped 30 times by his country, admitted the scenes at the end of the game soured the day in some ways for the Scotland players, whose success secured the Home Championship title that year. At the same time, he confessed, 'There's no doubt it was the highlight of my career. You always wanted to play for your country against England at Wembley – and beat them. I scored the first goal just before the break and Kenny Dalglish got the second in the second half. The fans went berserk at the end and everyone remembers the game for that. It was disappointing for the players because we'd won the Home Championship.'

Some have suggested that the fixture should be restored to the international calendar at the end of each season, but McQueen, speaking in 2014, said, 'Scotland-England games are nothing like they were. It's not the same as the days when the fans saved up for two years to go to Wembley, putting 50p or whatever in a tin each week. It's not the same any more – there are Champions League games and all sorts of other big matches. They've talked about bringing the Scotland-England fixture back as an annual thing, but I don't think it would work. I'm not sure that every England player would be up for it.'

Scotland skipper Rioch, a fiercely competitive midfielder, was hoisted on to the shoulders of the ecstatic Caledonian masses who swarmed all over Wembley, while Revie literally ran for cover and the sanctuary of the tunnel. Straight after the Scotland debacle, England's players had to lift themselves for the trip to South America. But to say that more trouble lay ahead would be a monumental understatement.

14

Desertion in the Desert

ONLY FOUR days after losing to Scotland, England faced Brazil in Rio de Janeiro on 8 June 1977, when Don Revie's trusted and loyal lieutenant, Les Cocker, took charge due to the manager's late arrival in South America. The sides played out a highly entertaining goalless stalemate and, though Brazil were ultimately the more threatening, England had their chances and it was a game which could have gone either way.

Ray Clemence and Trevor Cherry came to England's rescue, the keeper making key saves and the left-back – one of Revie's former Leeds charges – setting the tone for a prominent role on the tour by performing no fewer than three goal-line clearances as his side fought a determined rearguard action in the face of a Brazilian onslaught.

Then, with Revie back in harness, came a volatile 1-1 draw against Argentina at Boca Juniors' *La Bombonera* ('The Chocolate Box', due to its shape) in Buenos Aires, where, predictably between old foes, there was no sweetness and light as Cherry was harshly sent off after a clash with Daniel Bertoni in the closing stages of the match. Cherry, who had already been cautioned in the first half, appeared to be guilty of the initial foul, but Bertoni reacted with a punch which relieved the Englishman of two teeth. Both were dismissed by Uruguayan referee Ramón Barreto, with Cherry leaving the pitch under a hail of missiles from home supporters, and Revie was moved to say, 'Trevor is the unluckiest player in the world to be sent off.'

England were subjected to ironic cries of 'animals, animals' from the home fans in a reference to former manager Alf Ramsey's description of the Argentinians after the sides had met at the 1966 World Cup. In an eventful opening, however, the noisy crowd fell silent when striker Stuart Pearson headed a third-minute goal from Mick Channon's right-wing cross. Then Bertoni, who had been fouled by Brian Greenhoff, struck a cunning 15th-minute free kick to deliver a counter-punch of a different variety to the one he would later land on Cherry. The so-called friendly became a war of attrition until its explosive conclusion; England might have won the game late in the day when midfielder Ray Wilkins was through on goal but he had his shot saved by keeper Héctor Baley.

England rounded off their tour with another goalless draw, this time with Uruguay at the Estadio Centenario in Montevideo, where Revie – conscious of the need for goals in a World Cup qualifying context – bemoaned his side's deficiencies up front. He said, 'Our section will rest, I am sure, on goal difference and, at the moment, it is goals that are so hard to come by. We had 80 per cent of the game and controlled midfield, so it was disappointing not to win.' The fact that defender Cherry registered England's only shot on target said it all. What surprised Revie's men was the strangely restrained approach of the usually physical Uruguayans. Cherry said, 'It was almost as if they had been told to pull out and not get involved. We were surprised at how half-hearted some of their challenges were and I wish I could play against a winger as uncommitted as [Rudy]

Rodríguez every week – I could play until I was 50 if I did.' It was a repeat of the result in the opening match of the World Cup in 1966, but while that preceded far greater deeds, the encounter of '77 came a little under a month before one of the lowest points in England's history.

The foundations of the Football Association's Lancaster Gate headquarters were rocked when Revie, fearing he was facing the sack and with allegations of match-fixing in the wind from his time at Leeds, dramatically walked out on his country to take charge of the United Arab Emirates. It was a four-year deal worth what was then a hugely lucrative £340,000, tax-free – an astronomical hike on the £25,000 annual salary he was paid by the FA. It emerged later that, before he stood down, Revie sought a payoff from the FA to resign, covering the remaining two years on his contract, but they refused point-blank. The way in which he then departed provoked fury among English football's top brass as he sold his story to the *Daily Mail*, who published on 12 July, while his letter of resignation had not been seen by the FA because it arrived at their HQ the night before – but after they had closed for business. 'Revie quits over "Aggro"' was the headline on Jeff Powell's exclusive. 'I sat down with my wife, Elsie, one night and we agreed the job was no longer worth all the aggravation ... it was bringing too much heartache to those nearest to us,' said Revie. 'Nearly everyone in the country seems to want me out. I'm giving them what they want.' The next day, the *Mail*'s headline was 'Revie hits the jackpot' as they revealed the riches that awaited him in the Middle East.

Ostensibly, in leaving Cocker to oversee the Brazil game, Revie had been running the rule over World Cup group rivals Italy in their 3-0 qualifying win against Finland in Helsinki. It emerged, however, that he was in clandestine talks with the UAE, even reputedly adopting traditional Arab garb as a disguise at one point as part of the subterfuge, though Revie said his identity could only have been concealed by the sunglasses he wore. FA chairman Sir Harold Thompson, whose relationship with Ramsey had been testy, also had tetchy dealings with Revie. 'They genuinely hated each other,' said Revie's son, Duncan. 'Thompson was an old Corinthian who always treated the manager like a serf.' Once, at an official dinner, in a story recounted by many, Thompson said, 'When I get to know you better, Revie, I shall call you Don,' and Revie snapped back, 'When I get to know you better, Thompson, I shall call you Sir Harold.'

When the revelations over Revie's future came into the public domain, Thompson was incandescent with anger at what was seen, by the FA and beyond, as the manager's outright betrayal. FA secretary Ted Croker said, 'The committee unanimously deplores the action of Don Revie … and the FA is taking legal advice.' Alan Hardaker, Croker's opposite number at the Football League, was among those who had never made any attempt to hide disdain for Revie and needed no invitation to wade into the widespread condemnation of his actions. In a barbed reference to Revie's insistence on his England players taking part in games of bingo to pass the time, a sarcastic Hardaker said he hoped the exiting manager would soon learn how to call out the numbers in Arabic.

Revie was charged with bringing the game into disrepute, but it was more than a year after he had quit before a disciplinary hearing took place. The outcome was the imposition of a draconian decade-long ban from English football and the matter ended up in the High Court, where Revie successfully challenged his suspension, which was overturned as the FA were found to have acted beyond their jurisdiction. But Revie did not escape censure. Mr Justice Cantley said Revie's resignation had demonstrated a 'sensational, outrageous example of disloyalty, breach of trust, discourtesy and selfishness'.

It was claimed that the FA had already been sounding out potential replacements for Revie before his decision to go was splashed all over the national press. Ipswich manager Bobby Robson, who would become England's choice to succeed Ron Greenwood in 1982, was said to be one of those who were of interest to the FA as they eyed a replacement for Revie. Reputation is everything, and in his own country Revie's was past repair. He never worked in English football again. After his three years in charge of the UAE, he managed the country's Al-Nasr club for four years and Egypt's Al-Ahly briefly. By 1984, he had returned to the UK and it is believed that the closest he came to ending his football exile on home soil was when Queens Park Rangers chairman Jim Gregory approached him about replacing former England midfielder Alan Mullery as manager at Loftus Road. But there was no agreement and within five years Revie was dead. The devastating motor neurone disease claimed him at the age of 61 on 26 May 1989, but his passing was rather overshadowed as events at Anfield that night dominated the football headlines after Michael Thomas's last-gasp goal clinched the First Division title for Arsenal, who secured the 2-0 win they required to pip Liverpool to the crown in a remarkable climax to the season.

England's World Cup qualifying push in 1977 was bereft of such excitement, though with Revie long gone and Greenwood in charge they conjured up a notable November victory, beating Italy 2-0 at Wembley. It avenged the 2-0 defeat in Rome almost exactly a year earlier and lifted England to the top of the group, but self-inflicted wounds would not heal. Ultimately, their lack of goals against Finland and Luxembourg proved decisive as the Italians qualified.

Of Revie's 29 matches in charge, England won only 14 and drew eight. It was indicative of his chaotic reign and erratic selection policy that, under Revie, England used 52 players and dished out 29 new caps – an average of one every match – and only once did he name an unchanged side. The irony of those statistics would certainly have not been lost on his predecessor, Ramsey, given Revie's instinctive reluctance to release players for international duty during his time as manager of Leeds.

15

Keeping up Appearances

ON 27 May 1972, Gordon Banks, one of the undisputed greatest goalkeepers of all time, played his last game for England. What followed later that year was not the start of a struggle to fill the void he had left, rather an intense battle which would continue into the 1980s. Peter Shilton and Ray Clemence are two of the most revered names in British football. The fact that there was only a year between them in terms of age made the fight for the number one jersey all the more fascinating. There have, of course, been other occasions when a nation has had two outstanding keepers playing in the same era, with the competition between Oliver Kahn and Jens Lehmann in the Germany team of the 1990s genuinely comparable to the Shilton-Clemence rivalry.

Whenever a country has two world-class players in one position, there will always be those who miss out. Alex Stepney, Jimmy Rimmer and Phil Parkes, all accomplished keepers who had decorated careers, only won a cap apiece. Sunderland's Jim Montgomery, despite his heroics in the 1973 FA Cup Final, never played for England's senior team. Only one keeper other than Shilton and Clemence was under serious consideration by England's managers during the mid-to-late 1970s. Manchester City's Joe Corrigan was an outstanding shot-stopper who would have surely won more than his nine caps if he had been born in a different era; the fact that no one has played more for England's B team than him speaks volumes. Second on City's all-time appearances list, Corrigan was at the time one of the tallest players in the First Division and was remarkably agile for 6ft 4in. He would never feature in a major tournament for England, a large proportion of his international appearances coming in British Home Championships or in friendlies. Unfortunately for Corrigan, he just so happened to be born the same year as Clemence.

Like Kevin Keegan, Clemence began his professional career at Scunthorpe United. While at the Lincolnshire club, on occasion he worked as a deck-chair assistant at Skegness to boost his modest wages. Bill Shankly would oversee his move to Liverpool for £18,000 in 1967, and Clemence would go on to spend the next 14 years of his career at the club, collecting a winners' medal for every major trophy available to an English club side. He made his international debut in November 1972 during the season that climaxed with him winning his first league title with Liverpool. His standout moment for the club was arguably a great save from Uli Stielike in the European Cup Final win over Borussia Mönchengladbach in 1977 when the scores were still level at 1-1. Don Revie greatly favoured Clemence during his reign, though England's qualifying struggles during the era meant that he would never play in a World Cup finals match. In total, he was capped 61 times for England which places him ahead of fellow keepers David James and Paul Robinson. In 1981, with his game time limited due to the arrival of Bruce Grobbelaar, Clemence left Anfield to join Tottenham Hotspur where he enjoyed further successes. He is one of a select number of players to reach more than 1,000 professional appearances, the world record holder, of course, being Shilton.

Despite having had to engage in such a fierce duel for his place in the team, Shilton amassed a record 125 caps in a near-20-year England career before retiring from international duty after Italia '90. Starting as an understudy to Banks at Leicester City, Shilton made his professional debut at only 16 and his emergence and precocious ability spelled the end of the road at Filbert Street for the World Cup winner. The Foxes, prematurely most would say, decided that they could cash in on Banks, who was sold to Stoke City for £50,000 in 1967. Ironically, Shilton would follow in the footsteps of Banks yet again when he moved to the high-flying Potters, who missed out on the First Division title by just four points in the 1974/75 season. Financial issues then led to Shilton being sold to Nottingham Forest in 1977, and the move paid instant dividends. Under Brian Clough's stewardship, he would win two back-to-back European Cups in a five-year spell at the club. Later in his career he went on to turn out for Southampton and Derby County before becoming player-manager at Plymouth Argyle and then drifting to several other clubs as his playing days wound down. In a remarkable career which lasted more than 30 years, Shilton won numerous trophies, yet the FA Cup eluded him: he was on the losing side with Leicester against Manchester City in 1969.

In part due to his longevity, Shilton won more than twice as many England caps as Clemence, as he ultimately wrested control of the goalkeeper jersey. It will forever remain open to debate whether Clemence should have featured more for the national team, his last appearance coming in 1983. Few, however, would argue against Clemence being a better penalty-stopper than his rival. Incredibly, Shilton only saved a single penalty for England, while there is an urban legend that Bobby Robson was considering substituting him before the shoot-out of the 1990 World Cup semi-final against

Emlyn Hughes (left), Geoff Hurst (centre) and Jeff Astle at Heathrow Airport before England head to the 1970 World Cup in Mexico.

England captain Bobby Moore and Brazil star Pelé exchange shirts in a moment of mutual respect after their World Cup duel in Guadalajara.

Extra time looms in the World Cup quarter-final against West Germany as Bobby Charlton (left), who had been substituted by Colin Bell (right), feels the heat along with Brian Labone (front).

Roy McFarland (left) and Rodney Marsh in an aerial challenge with West Germany goalkeeper Sepp Maier in the 1972 European Championship quarter-final, second leg in Berlin, with the hosts' Paul Breitner (no 3) looking on.

Mick Channon (extreme left) goes agonisingly close to scoring against Poland at Wembley in 1973 in one of many frustrating moments for England as they fail to qualify for the World Cup.

Goalkeeper Gordon Banks takes a goal kick against Wales in the Home Championship at Cardiff's Ninian Park in 1972 in what proved to be his penultimate appearance for England.

Sir Alf Ramsey, pictured in 1973, the year that would witness the beginning of the end of his World Cup-winning reign as England manager.

England caretaker manager Joe Mercer (left), and backroom men Harold Shepherdson (centre) and Les Cocker during training at Roehampton in 1974.

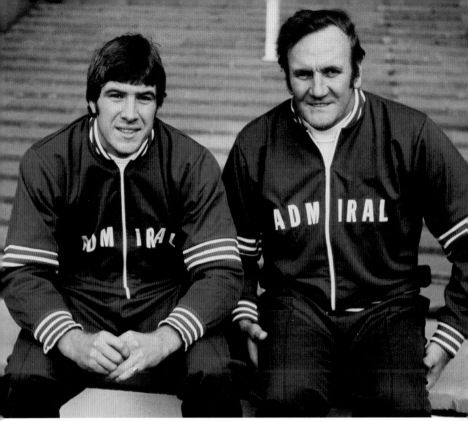

Captain and manager Emlyn Hughes and Don Revie at Wembley in October 1974, two days before the former Leeds boss took charge of an England game for the first time, winning 3-0 at home to Czechoslovakia.

Malcolm Macdonald celebrates after scoring the first of his five goals against Cyprus in a European Championship qualifier at Wembley in April 1975.

Frank Worthington goes up for the ball with Argentina's Ángel Bargas (no 6) and Agus Balbuena at Wembley in May 1974.

Mick Channon tries to go between Scotland defenders Gordon McQueen (left) and Francis Munro in a Home Championship clash at Wembley in 1975.

Joe Corrigan (left), Peter Shilton (centre) and Ray Clemence show their hands in the battle to be England's first-choice keeper as they await departure at Luton Airport for the game in Bulgaria in June 1979.

Ron Greenwood talks to his players during training before the friendly game with West Germany in Munich in February 1978.

England captain Kevin Keegan, who became Britain's most expensive player when he joined Hamburg for £500,000 in 1977, in action for the Bundesliga side in March 1979.

Right-back Viv Anderson lines up before his historic England debut against Czechoslovakia at Wembley in November 1978.

West Germany for Dave Beasant – who was not even on the bench that fateful evening. In terms of clean sheets – widely considered the best statistic to judge a goalkeeper's ability – Shilton managed 66 to Clemence's 27, which after taking into account the former's greater number of caps shows that, on average, he only bettered him in this department by a relatively small margin.

* * *

In the wake of Revie's shocking departure, the FA turned to a favourite of theirs to take up caretaking responsibilities. One of the running themes of Ron Greenwood's tenure as England manager was his inclination to frequently rotate between Shilton and Clemence. Though that could be seen as indecision, Greenwood was in fairness presented with a predicament which no manager past or present could have handled much differently. Between mid-1974 and 1977, Shilton had, in fact, barely featured which could lead to suggest that the infamous Poland games, where he hardly covered himself in glory, had played a part in his prolonged exclusion from Revie's team sheet.

For his first match, a friendly at home to Switzerland on 7 September 1977, Greenwood opted to continue with Clemence. The game was a dour affair and it is best remembered not for being Greenwood's debut as England manager, but rather for the fact that over half of the players he fielded played for the same club. Midfielder Terry McDermott explained, 'I remember Ron Greenwood naming six Liverpool players in his England team. I was one of them, and it was my debut. Ray Clemence, Phil Neal, Emlyn Hughes, Ray Kennedy and Ian Callaghan were the others. Kevin Keegan, who had just left us to go to Hamburg, was in the side, too. And we drew 0-0 with Switzerland in a friendly match at Wembley. So that wasn't a good experiment, was it? Even with six team-mates, it was difficult to gel. But it's different playing for your country compared to playing for your club.' Though Greenwood's experiment did not pay off, it was on paper a reasonable idea as Liverpool were one of the dominant forces in European football in the late '70s, and the friendly was also a fair opportunity to tinker with an underperforming side.

Although the game marked the start of the road for some, it was the end of the line for Mick Channon, who made his last appearance in an England shirt. Out of all the players who made their England debuts in the 1970s, Channon ties with Keegan in terms of goals. Both players found the net 21 times, Channon's goals coming in only 46 appearances. By discarding the then-28-year-old, Greenwood showed that he was prepared to be ruthless as he began to reshape his squad with younger attackers such as Trevor Francis, Paul Mariner, Bob Latchford and, before too long, Tony Woodcock coming into the fold. Despite the fact that Channon was to have a mediocre season by his standards at Manchester City following his £300,000 transfer from Southampton in the summer of 1977, the decision to never field him for England again was harsh in retrospect, especially considering none of the aforementioned players would come close to his international goal haul. Channon, who went on to have an enormously successful career as a racehorse trainer, remains the most-capped England player never to appear at a major tournament. At 21, he was a little too young, and up against great competition, to make England's 1970 World Cup squad – his debut did not come until over two years later – and the failures to qualify for the 1974 edition and the business end of the 1976 European Championship compounded Channon's frustration.

It was not so much 'out with the old and in with the new' where Ian Callaghan was concerned. Unquestionably in the pantheon of Liverpool greats, Callaghan had last played for England during the 1966 World Cup and, at the age of 35, made a shock return to international duty for the game with the Swiss. In many ways he was the odd player out in an otherwise youthful side, though he had evidently impressed Greenwood greatly through his displays in the European Cup. This Indian summer would be short-lived. After featuring in Greenwood's first two games, Callaghan would not play for England again and went on to finish his playing career three years later. When aged 67, however, he did receive yet another medal. Only those who had played in the final of 1966 had initially been awarded medals, and after a long campaign Callaghan finally received the honour in 2009.

In the wake of the Switzerland game, and with one eye on his squad for the must-win World Cup qualifier in Luxembourg on 12 October, one of the matches Greenwood took in was Queens Park Rangers at home to Manchester City. Gerry Francis, QPR's midfield fulcrum, had not played for England since the 4-1 qualifying win in Finland in the summer of 1976 after having seemingly become indispensable to Revie. There was talk of an England recall for Francis; yet, despite an outstanding display in which he scored his side's equaliser in a 1-1 draw, there were to be no more caps. The only player to face Luxembourg after being on show at Loftus Road was City centre-back Dave Watson, who by then had already cemented his place with England. Team-mate Peter Barnes, however, had clearly made an impression on Greenwood's trip to Shepherd's Bush as the winger would soon make his England debut.

Clemence had put in a solid performance against Switzerland and he resumed in Luxembourg after overcoming a swollen wrist sustained with Liverpool in their 2-0 win over Chelsea. At one stage, he was rated doubtful, but his recovery meant there was only one player fewer from Liverpool in the side with Phil Neal missing. Uncapped Trevor Whymark, of Ipswich Town, was named on the bench along with his club-mate Kevin Beattie. Coming into the match, England were acutely aware that the Italians had a game in hand on them and that nothing other than a goal glut against Luxembourg would be deemed an acceptable result. Deep down, Greenwood was conscious that, irrespective of how many goals England scored, the odds were still very much stacked against them in terms of their prospects of World Cup qualification.

Even if that feeling had transmitted to the players, they would have been mindful themselves that there was a real chance it was a lost cause. Nevertheless, England's attacking intent was there for all to see in that Greenwood only named three defenders – Watson, Trevor Cherry and Emlyn Hughes – in his starting line-up. The deadlock was broken in the 30th minute when Ray Kennedy scored his third goal for his country. Chance after chance was then squandered in a thoroughly frustrating game which could be regarded as one of the nation's worst-ever wins. Even Mariner's first international goal, scored in added time, could not mask the poor performance in the 2-0 win. Keegan had been unavailable due to personal reasons, while Channon, of course, who had scored twice in the reverse fixture against Luxembourg, was also missing. Greenwood's gambit in fielding a relatively inexperienced, albeit attacking side, had failed.

Three days later, Italy dispatched Finland 6-1 in Turin, and Greenwood, who was in attendance, was forced to concede, 'We lost this section a year ago in Rome. I cannot see Italy failing to go forward to Argentina. They are an improving side, almost as strong as West Germany.' He added, 'We needed a miracle today – like Finland taking a point. Instead, we saw a clinical destruction.' Greenwood was also asked about his future and insisted he was still in the dark, saying, 'I know nothing. I haven't spoken to the FA about the situation and they haven't spoken to me. I'm waiting for a proposition.' Roberto Bettega bagged four goals for Italy, which left England needing to not only beat them by a comfortable margin in their next game, but also hope the *Azzurri* would slip up against Luxembourg in the final match of the group, a notion that Greenwood dismissed as 'ridiculous'. Enzo Bearzot's side were entertaining, solid defensively and had their own star keeper in Dino Zoff. The strength of the Italian side was predicated on the presence of key players from back-to-back *scudetto* winners Juventus – champions of Italy in 1977 and 1978 – with Zoff, defender Claudio Gentile, the versatile Marco Tardelli, midfielder Romeo Benetti, winger Franco Causio and forward Bettega all lining up at Wembley, where Juve's defender-cum-midfielder Antonello Cuccureddu came on as a substitute. There was a mixture of silk and steel, and in defence a little more sophistication than opponents had been used to from some of the brutal Italy sides of earlier years.

To combat this skilful and confident side, Greenwood made drastic alterations to his line-up with three debutants given an opportunity to impress. The inclusion of Latchford was arguably overdue – there had already been calls for him to play for England during Revie's term and he had staked his claim by hitting four goals for Everton in their 5-1 win at QPR shortly before the game in Luxembourg. But the barrel-chested centre-forward would become a mainstay in the England side until mid-1979 in what was a short but impressive international career. Having transferred from Birmingham City in 1974, Latchford would also prove to be one of Everton's all-time great goalscorers. The youngest of the three uncapped players was Barnes, who had been named as the PFA Young Player of the Year the previous season, so there were few eyebrows raised when the winger received his call-up. Steve Coppell was the final member of the trio. Dependable and creative, the Liverpudlian had been plucked by Manchester United from Tranmere Rovers two years earlier and had helped United lift the FA Cup and the Charity Shield in 1977. Coppell would win 42 caps for England and also featured in more than 300 games for United, though he would have surely played more for both sides if it had not been for a serious injury. The decision by Greenwood to opt for the debutants in a vital match was all the more bold as there were many established attackers in the First Division who were in good form, including Arsenal's Malcolm Macdonald and Manchester City pair Brian Kidd and Dennis Tueart.

Most of the attention on the day, however, was on the one English player who could offer a glimmer of hope against the seemingly insurmountable odds. The return of England's talisman, Kevin Keegan, was most welcome, and his performance in the game would once more highlight his importance to the team. In the 11th minute, Trevor Brooking whipped the ball into the box from the right wing and Keegan pulled away from his marker before finding the net with an expertly directed header to place his team one up. For a player who was only 5ft 8in, Keegan had an impressive knack of scoring headers, and this record had much to do with his movement off the ball. During the match it became clear that the Italians had devised an underhanded game plan to stifle the Hamburg forward. Tardelli provided the most controversial moment of the game when he elbowed Keegan in the face while they were running for the ball, an incident the referee missed entirely. Much to the chagrin of the England fans, Keegan was booked soon afterwards for an innocuous shove on Tardelli. The Italians were rattled by the early goal, fearful that a drubbing could leave qualification in the balance. Barnes was guilty of missing a great chance to unnerve England's opponents further in the first half when the winger hit his volley into the ground, a shot which left Zoff untroubled as he watched the ball bounce out of play for a goal kick. Later, Barnes nearly atoned for the miss after a brilliant jinking run into the box, but his shot was from a tight angle and Zoff was able to make a routine stop.

Despite the number of good attacking players at their disposal, Italy would offer little in the way of forward threat, seemingly content with slowing down play while keeping the deficit respectable. Greenwood revealed after the game that his side had identified Zoff's throws as an important source of Italy's build-up play, so they had employed a tactic which pressured the keeper. England continued to search for further opportunities to breach the blue wall, yet strong defensive play from the Italian back line limited Greenwood's men predominantly to half-chances. They threw on Manchester United's Stuart Pearson – who had immortalised himself with the Old Trafford faithful six months earlier by scoring in their FA Cup Final triumph over Liverpool – for Latchford in the 75th minute in an attempt to inject some energy to their flagging attack. Eventually, England were able to find the net once more when Keegan played a defence-splitting pass which found Brooking. The West Ham man had slipped into the box unnoticed by the Italians in a rare lapse of concentration, and Brooking coolly placed the ball into the bottom corner for his first international goal. In his autobiography *My Life in Football*, Keegan quipped, 'He would have to forgive me for not joining in the celebrations because, as he was tucking the ball past Dino Zoff, I was lying on the turf in a crumpled heap. Benetti had seen his chance, waited for me to play the pass and cleaned me out.' Having suffered a knee injury, Keegan was unable to last the whole 90 minutes and departed late on for Trevor Francis.

The final whistle signalled the end of England's campaign, though it had not officially confirmed their fate. With the top two teams level on goal difference, Italy needed only to beat Luxembourg – which they did, 3-0 in Rome – to make it to Argentina. Viewing England's 2-0 win in isolation, there was much for Greenwood to be optimistic about and, in his autobiography *Yours Sincerely*, he hailed the victory 'a wonderful shot in the arm', adding, 'Coppell and Barnes were essential to the pattern and I believed they were part of England's long-term future. They gave us width and flair, they were the edge to our blade, and I would keep them in the team as long as I was in charge.' Keegan's showing had also been particularly pleasing. Having only scored five times under Revie, the forward would find a new lease of life under Greenwood, a manager who was happy to let Keegan express himself rather than bog him down in opposition dossiers. Clemence had also achieved his fourth clean sheet in a row, though the Liverpool man had admittedly seldom been called into action during these outings thanks to his team-mates. The year of 1977 would mark the end of Clemence's prolonged spell as England's first-choice keeper, as Shilton and Corrigan gradually began to pick up more game time.

Unbeknown to all who were among the crowd, there was a future England World Cup manager sitting on the bench, though he was not in the home dugout. Fabio Capello was an unused squad member on the night and was in the twilight years of his playing career at AC Milan, the club where he would start his training to be a coach. Greenwood and Capello would lead the Three Lions to one World Cup each (1982 and 2010 respectively), and they also both failed to make it past the second round of the competition. Qualifying for a World Cup may well have felt like a pipe dream to many who watched their team trudge off the Wembley pitch that November evening. This would be Greenwood's last match as caretaker manager. Unlike the drawn-out affair that was Revie's appointment, the FA would act quickly in installing a new coach. Greenwood, tasked with turning around England's fortunes, had already begun in earnest shaping the side for a new era.

16

A Safe Pair of Hands

EVEN AN extraordinary scandal such as the one that led to Don Revie's departure did not distract the fans from the overriding question: who was to be England's next manager? The obvious candidate was Revie's nemesis. Many people to this day believe that Brian Clough should have been appointed in 1977. On Clough's interview for the role, FA panel member Peter Swales said, 'He gave by far the best interview of all the candidates – confident, passionate, full of common sense and above all patriotic. If Ron Greenwood hadn't been around, he'd have clinched it.'

The truth was that the FA were wary of Clough. Never part of the establishment, the then-Nottingham Forest boss was a larger-than-life character who was always unafraid to speak his mind. His tenure at Leeds United, lasting only 44 days and during which he fell out with most of his playing staff, remains one of the most infamous football stories, and the debacle was surely at the forefront of the minds of the five-man panel when they sat down with him. Clough and Greenwood were not the only high-profile managers considered by the FA. Future England boss Bobby Robson, then of Ipswich, and Southampton's Lawrie McMenemy, who became the national side's number two under Graham

Taylor in the 1990s, were among those discussed along with, surprisingly, respected FA coach Allen Wade. Robson was even the favourite with the bookmakers at one stage. In spite of the short odds briefly offered on him landing the job, England's 2-0 win over Italy, with Greenwood acting as caretaker manager, meant that, by November 1977, the contest for the post had practically become a two-horse race.

After their disastrous decision to appoint Revie, Greenwood was seen by the FA as a safe pair of hands. In this regard, the situation was not entirely dissimilar to how future FA chairman David Bernstein selected the experienced Roy Hodgson to take over the national team in 2012. Another factor which added weight to Greenwood's credentials was that he had been instrumental in developing World Cup-winning trio Bobby Moore, Geoff Hurst and Martin Peters at West Ham. Greenwood had, in fact, been under consideration for the role as early as 1962 before the FA made undoubtedly the right decision in selecting Alf Ramsey.

As a player, Greenwood had enjoyed a successful career, winning the First Division with Chelsea in the 1954/55 season, though he never appeared for England's senior team. The closest the centre-half came to winning a cap was his sole outing for England's B side in 1952. He had completed his coaching badge soon after his retirement as a player and coached Oxford University's team as well as England under-21s. After a spell as Arsenal's assistant manager, his big break came when he was appointed as West Ham manager in 1961. His decision to build his team around homegrown talent, and the culture he instilled at Upton Park for nurturing young players, led to the Hammers being dubbed 'The Academy'. In his 13-year spell in charge – after which he became general manager for three years with John Lyall succeeding him as team boss – West Ham won their first major silverware, lifting the FA Cup in 1964 and the European Cup Winners'

Cup a year later. Greenwood is, of course, lauded as arguably their greatest manager. It is perhaps surprising to note, however, that the highest league placing he achieved at the club was during the 1972/73 season when they finished sixth in the First Division.

A devoted footballing purist with acute tactical acumen, Greenwood expected his teams to play in an aesthetically pleasing style. Forward Bryan 'Pop' Robson, whose career is featured in Chapter 19, played under Greenwood at West Ham. Robson said, 'He was very positive. We played really good football, moved the ball quickly and it was really exciting. The passing at times was one-touch, two-touch, making angles and third-man running. The full-backs would attack. Bobby Moore would sometimes come and play in front of the defence and distribute passes. We did create a lot of chances. Sometimes we would concede one or two goals but it was really enjoyable. Ron was a great coach and the training was always nice and bright. I think he didn't get the credit he deserved. John Lyall, who worked under him, was also an excellent coach. John went on to win the FA Cup a couple of times as manager.

'There were some good players at West Ham. Bobby Moore was obviously the standout, and there was Geoff Hurst. But they also had the likes of Billy Bonds and Trevor Brooking. Hursty was a fantastic target man. It was a case of hitting the front players early, but they were quality balls, not just up in the air all the time. It was dropping balls in short. It wasn't an accident that they were good players. They'd been well coached and well drilled and we spent a lot of time on near-post crosses. The ball that Bobby Moore knocked in quickly to Geoff Hurst in the World Cup Final … he just put the ball down and Hursty got on the end of it. We worked on those sort of things in training and it was fantastic. I enjoyed it at West Ham and I scored a lot of goals. When I went back for my second spell there, John had taken over as manager and Ron was general manager and a little bit in the background, but he was still there to advise you. As a coach, he was always creative. England played good football under Ron as well, and he had Trevor who linked up well with Kevin Keegan.'

There was a contrast in many ways with Revie's rugged, results-driven approach to the game, albeit that Greenwood's predecessor always demanded that his sides entertained and attacked with potent flair. One of the starkest differences between them was that, while Revie constantly shuffled his pack, Greenwood strove for a settled side and that desire led to the end of some international careers. Centre-back Mike Doyle, utility player Paul Madeley and winger Peter Taylor did not play for England again following Revie's departure and Kevin Beattie only appeared once more. In the case of Ipswich's Beattie, however, the cultured and versatile defender would have surely won more than his nine caps if it had not been for a series of injuries.

A little over a week before Greenwood's appointment was confirmed on 12 December 1977, England's World Cup fate was also sealed. The win over Italy had meant that they were not officially out of the race for qualification, yet in reality this was a stay of execution as the *Azzurri*'s game in hand was at home to Luxembourg, who had lost all their group matches up to that point. The probability that the minnows could shut out a team that featured forwards of the quality of Roberto Bettega and Francesco Graziani was astronomically unlikely, and the only surprise when Italy won 3-0 was that they had not scored more. England finished second in the final standings of the qualifying group on goal difference. No one who had watched Moore lift the Jules Rimet Trophy 11 years previously would have thought for a moment that such a barren period could lie ahead for England in terms of being involved in major tournaments. It should be highlighted, however, that their route to the 1978 World Cup was one of the most difficult they have ever faced. In comparison, England made it to Brazil in 1950 and Switzerland in 1954 by winning British Home Championships, while they qualified as hosts in 1966 and holders in 1970. Disregarding Finland and Luxembourg due to their lack of genuine quality, England were effectively in a straight fight with a football superpower in Italy.

Greenwood's chief objective was to restore some pride and there was only one way he could achieve this: reach a major competition. England's next fixture was an away friendly against West Germany in a packed Olympiastadion in Munich. The Germans fielded a mixture of experience and youth with veterans like goalkeeper Sepp Maier and defender Berti Vogts alongside the up-and-coming striker Karl-Heinz Rummenigge. England only made two changes to their starting line-up from the Italy game, defender Trevor Cherry and striker Bob Latchford making way for Mick Mills and Stuart Pearson. There was no shame in their 2-1 loss, but the manner of the defeat was disappointing after England had gone in at half-time with a 1-0 lead thanks to a clever looping header from Pearson. They led until the 75th minute when Ronald Worm burst down the left flank and finished, his shot agonisingly squeezing under the diving Ray Clemence. The winner was cruel on England. In the 85th minute, defender Dave Watson gave away a contentious foul almost 30 yards from goal and Rainer Bonhof struck home a low drive direct from the free kick, leaving England infuriated and complaining bitterly to the referee. England had the right to feel hard done by, though they could also be content that they had given the world champions a stern examination.

On paper, their next opponents presented slightly less of a challenge, but nevertheless came with a considerable reputation. Most of Brazil's 1970 World Cup-winning squad had now retired, and they were going through a transitional period. They could, however, still rely on three players from 1970 with playmaker Rivelino, defender Zé Maria and goalkeeper Émerson Leão – understudy to Félix in Mexico eight years earlier – all on show. They also had the skilful Zico in tremendous form. The friendly on 19 April 1978 at Wembley was a very different game to England's fixture against West Germany two months earlier. Greenwood said, 'I think the nicest thing we can say is that Brazil were over-physical because we caused them a lot of problems. We have always looked upon the yellow shirt of Brazil as something a little magical. But if they play like that in the World Cup, I don't think they will be very successful. I like to think that it was the fact that we caused them a lot of problems that made Brazil resort to dubious tactics. Personally, I do not wish to play football like that. If they want to play it that way, that's their problem.'

There was, though, a flash of the old Brazil in their goal: Gil cut inside from the right, and although Cherry was able to stay with him, the attacker struck a powerful shot which beat the recalled Joe Corrigan. Owing to the unpleasant nature of the game – Brazil had five players booked – Kevin Keegan's equaliser in the 70th minute was all the more sweet. The Hamburg forward scored from a powerful free kick which he blasted straight at Leão. The game finished 1-1, and there were clear signs that the new-look England side were starting to take shape. For the second game running, however, they could feel that luck had not been on their side. Latchford, winning his second cap, had put the ball in the net just before half-time only for the whistle to be blown for a foul on Leão, the keeper going down under minimal contact. Brazil would go on to finish the World Cup of 1978 undefeated, beating Italy in the third-place match.

Greenwood's attention turned to his only opportunity of silverware that year: in the Home Championship. Some performances in the competition had bordered on embarrassing under Revie, and England were now desperate to bring the trophy south of the border for the first time in two years. First up were Wales at Ninian Park on 13 May. England started strongly, Latchford scoring his first international goal in the eighth minute, but a reply from Cardiff City defender Phil Dwyer in the second half set up a tense finale. Tony Currie, who had come on for Latchford after the Everton forward suffered an injury, settled English nerves with a brilliant finish from well outside the box, the shot curling into the top corner of the net. The contest was ended by Peter Barnes with another great England goal which went in off the underside of the crossbar. England had been far from at their best, and the lateness of their second and third goals (which both came in the last ten minutes of normal time) was testament to this, even though they had been impressive for long spells in the game. Unfortunately, the win had come at a cost: Cherry had broken his collarbone early on in the game and was ruled out of the remainder of the competition.

Their next game was three days later at home to Northern Ireland. Thanks to a goal from Martin O'Neill, the Irish had drawn 1-1 against Scotland in their opening game of the Home Championship, meaning England had an excellent chance to cement their position at the top of the table. Phil Neal had a happy habit of scoring important goals for both club and country – the fact that he took penalties helped – and the Liverpool legend opened his England account with a goal more befitting of a striker than a full-back. Deep into the Irish half, Neal stroked the ball home with precision after receiving a knock-down from Watson a minute before half-time. The game ended 1-0 to England, while Wales and

Scotland cancelled each other out in their match. In modern times, these results would have meant that the Three Lions had an unassailable lead over their rivals. However, wins were still only worth two points in the late 1970s, leaving England needing at least a draw to be confirmed as champions.

Scotland had much to brag about in the build-up to the showdown at Hampden Park on 20 May. Not only did they have several outstanding players at their disposal, they had also – unlike England – qualified for the World Cup in Argentina. Although they had performed below par in their last two games, Scotland were still confident that they could overpower their great rivals in front of a capacity crowd. Graeme Souness and Archie Gemmill both started on the bench for Scotland, while Greenwood brought Trevor Francis, Paul Mariner and Barnes back into the fold. The Scots had the better chances of the two sides in a busy first half for Clemence, Manchester City midfielder Asa Hartford squandering a golden opportunity when he broke free of the England defence and dragged his shot wide. The small number of England fans in the ground were jubilant when Steve Coppell scored from a brilliant cross by Barnes seven minutes before the final whistle. Scotland continued to press until the end, Hartford coming the closest from a stooping header, but England held on. There was more than a hint of bitterness when Ally MacLeod declared, 'The worst player scored from a cross by the second worst player.' This was Scotland's last game before boarding the plane for Argentina, and they carried their indifferent form with them, losing their World Cup opener 3-1 against Peru.

England had regained the Home Championship title with a flawless record and having scored five times (all of the goals coming from different scorers) and conceded just once. By winning the tournament, Greenwood had equalled his predecessor's achievements with the England team in a matter of months. His faith in youngsters such as Coppell and Barnes had paid instant dividends, and there had been more than a glimmer of unity present in the way his team had played.

Their final game in what had been a busy month for the team was a friendly against Hungary. Since the war, England's record against the Magyars had been poor, though they had at least won their last encounter against them in 1965 thanks to a winner from Jimmy Greaves. England were boosted by the return of Keegan, one of only three changes to the side that started the Scotland game. England were the dominant force from the outset and raced into a lead within ten minutes when Keegan found Barnes in the box, the Manchester City man scoring a tame yet clever effort which trickled into the net. A dubious penalty was then awarded which was hammered home by Neal, before Trevor Francis found the net with a header. This third goal had come from a free kick which was given when Sándor Gujdár, the Hungarian keeper, cynically handled the ball way outside his area to deny the onrushing Keegan, an offence that, in modern times, certainly would have merited a red card. England eased up during the second period and László Nagy pulled a goal back for his side with a terrific first-time finish. Currie, only used once under Revie, ended the game as a contest 15 minutes later with a tremendous goal from 20 yards out.

Though by the 1970s the Hungarians no longer had players of the same class as greats like Ferenc Puskás and Nándor Hidegkuti, they were a competent side who had booked their place in Argentina by beating Bolivia in a UEFA-CONMEBOL play-off, and the fact that England had dispatched them 4-1 was a further indication that Greenwood's men were on the right path to once more becoming an international force. In his autobiography, *Yours Sincerely*, Greenwood said, 'I could see shape and promise in my squad: it had balance and healthy cover ... it did not have an orthodox British centre-forward but Francis and Keegan gave us pace and high mobility in the middle, Coppell and Barnes provided essential width and [Trevor] Brooking and [Ray] Wilkins had the ideas and patience to keep the whole machine ticking smoothly.' It had been England's biggest win in over a year, and the match acted as a good warm-up to the qualifying campaign of Euro 1980.

The headlines regarding English clubs during the 1977/78 season were dominated by three trophy winners. Having been promoted the season before, Nottingham Forest won not only the First Division title but also the League Cup in an incredible double for Clough's East Midlands side. Liverpool may have missed out on the English title that year, but the Anfield faithful were not too irked as they lifted the European Cup for a second successive year. Meanwhile, Ipswich defeated Arsenal in the FA Cup Final, a certain Bobby Robson masterminding the win. Unsurprisingly, many players from these three sides featured for the national team in that period. Away from the cup-winning exploits, Everton's Latchford was confirmed as the most deadly marksman in the country by topping the top-flight scoring charts with 30 goals, while there was a shock return to management for Ramsey at Birmingham City.

Next up for England were Denmark on 20 September in Copenhagen. This was Greenwood's first European Championship qualifier in a tough group which also included Bulgaria, Northern Ireland and the Republic of Ireland. In an exciting encounter which England won 4-3, Keegan put in a performance which showcased him as a complete player, scoring two well-timed headers in the space of five minutes. Denmark fought back and were level at the break with two quick-fire goals, capitalising on an unusually disorganised England back line. Allan Simonsen converted a penalty and

Frank Arnesen equalised. The Three Lions regained the lead through Latchford with yet another headed goal, but a fantastic finish by Neal that put England two goals to the good again was not enough to discourage the Danes, and the home side hit back, Per Røntved making for a nervy last five minutes. England had managed to register four goals in back-to-back games and they had also continued their scoring run which stretched back to the goalless draw against Switzerland over a year before.

Though the manner of the three goals they had conceded in Copenhagen was disappointing, Greenwood kept the same defence for their trip to face the Republic of Ireland in Dublin on 25 October. The game – one of only two encounters between the nations in the 1970s – took place against the backdrop of the ongoing Troubles. In February that year, the La Mon restaurant in Belfast had been bombed by the IRA, and the atrocity – which claimed 12 lives – was, of course, on the minds of the 48,000 who attended the match at Lansdowne Road. England took an early lead through Latchford, but the Republic were an equal match, Gerry Daly taking the scores level just before the half-hour mark. The Irish had several talented players, among them Arsenal's gifted midfielder Liam Brady, and the 1-1 draw was likely a fair result as both sides had a number of opportunities to grab a winner in what had been yet another end-to-end encounter for England. But Greenwood felt his side should have won, insisting, 'I thought we really bossed it in the second half. The disappointing thing is that we didn't make the most of the chances we created. We failed to punish them. You can blame that on bad shooting and their goalkeeper, Mick Kearns, who made some outstanding saves.'

This match, and the one preceding it, had also made it apparent that England were not the finished article defensively with issues becoming even clearer on the occasions they had to face sustained pressure. Ray Wilkins was a willing worker and did his part in screening the back line, though Greenwood encouraged the rest of his midfield to play high up the pitch, meaning opposition players did not have great difficulty finding pockets of space. This is not, however, to say that England's defence was a major concern: the players remained very mobile as a unit and were also strong aerially. A win and a draw from two tricky, away qualifiers was a decent start to the campaign for Greenwood's men, the results standing them in good stead for the remaining six games. With four of these fixtures due to take place at Wembley, there was plenty of confidence that England could finally end their tournament exile.

17

Equal Opportunities?

ARTHUR WHARTON, widely regarded as the first black professional footballer, began his career as an amateur at Darlington in 1885. More than 90 years later, Viv Anderson became the first black player to represent England's senior team.

The demographic of the country changed immeasurably in the decades that followed the end of World War Two, but it is impossible to escape the distinct impression that racism was one of the main reasons why it took until the late 1970s for England to have a black player in their side. One infamous case of discrimination in English football occurred when Plymouth Argyle inside-left Jack Leslie received a call-up in 1925. Leslie was at that time enjoying a free-scoring season in what was then the Third Division South. When the selectors discovered that the player in question was black, Leslie was deselected from the England squad to face Ireland and instead turned out for his club side on the day of the game. Leslie never received another call-up, but in 2023 he was posthumously awarded an honorary cap by the FA. In a slight twist of fate, a future England manager would call upon his services – but not as a player. Ron Greenwood recruited Leslie to work in West Ham's boot room where the former Plymouth man would go on to assist the likes of Bobby Moore and Trevor Brooking. It would not be until 1968 that England fielded their first player of a mixed ethnic background when Leeds United right-back Paul Reaney won the first of his three caps, coming on as a substitute in a 1-1 draw with Bulgaria at Wembley. Reaney would probably have been selected for England's 1970 World Cup squad if he had not broken his leg the same year.

Anderson came up through the ranks at Nottingham Forest and, after making his debut in 1974, he soon established himself as their first-choice right-back, helping them achieve promotion to the First Division in the 1976/77 season. Like all black players of the era, Anderson suffered terrible abuse from the stands. In one incident during a match at Carlisle, he cut short his warm-up as a substitute after having fruit hurled at him from the crowd. The response of Forest manager Brian Clough was to ask his defender to go back and pick him up 'two pears and a banana'. Anderson later recalled that Clough told him in the dressing room afterwards, 'If you let them dictate to you, you aren't going to make a good career and I think you can play. Don't let them influence you in any way.' Clough, renowned for batting away whatever criticism came his own way, proved to be a good mentor to the young Anderson.

Forest defeated Bob Paisley's Liverpool in a replay on 22 March 1978 to win the League Cup, by which time Anderson was firmly on England's radar. It is apt that, of all those who have managed England, it would be Greenwood who first named a black player in his side because, when at West Ham, he helped to develop the likes of Bermuda striker Clyde Best,

London-born John Charles,[1] his brother and fellow defender Clive Charles, and Nigerian-American forward Ade Coker in a time when practically every top-flight team had only white players in their squads. When discussing Anderson's call-up, Greenwood remarked, 'Yellow, purple or black – if they're good enough, I'll pick them.' In retrospect, the comment comes across as clumsy to say the least, though the underlying message was clearly well meaning.

If it had not been for Anderson's debut, the match itself, a friendly, may have gone down as one of the most forgettable of the era. The opponents were Czechoslovakia who, like England, had failed to qualify for that year's World Cup. The game presented England with an opportunity to avenge their 2-1 loss to the Czechoslovaks in 1975, a defeat which ultimately cost them dearly. It was little comfort to England fans that the side which pipped them to qualification for the European Championship would go on to win the tournament. Czechoslovakia's starting line-up which faced England at Wembley on 29 November was much changed from the side that had defeated West Germany on penalties. One of those who did feature in both fixtures was Antonín Panenka. Scorer of the winning penalty in the European Championship Final – converted using a technique which to this day carries his name – Panenka came on as a late substitute as his side fell to a 1-0 defeat on a frozen pitch at Wembley. As a spectacle, the game was greatly hampered by the conditions, and the outcome was settled by a scruffy goal from Steve Coppell in the 69th minute with Anderson involved in the build-

---

1   There is an ongoing debate as to who was the first black footballer to play for England at any level. John Charles played for England under-23s in the 1960s, while Benjamin Odeje – who was a youth player at Charlton Athletic – represented England Schoolboys in 1971. This chapter focuses on the men's senior side, yet both Charles and Odeje must be acknowledged due to their significant roles in English football history.

up. Greenwood used the friendly to experiment with his defence, Dave Watson the only one of the back four to have started the game against the Republic of Ireland the previous month. In the seemingly endless battle for the number one jersey, Peter Shilton came in for Ray Clemence. Along with Anderson and Shilton, another Forest player to play against the Czechoslovaks was Tony Woodcock, but his appearance was cut short through injury in the 36th minute.

Though England's year ended in a rather drab affair, many were likely to have been content with their record in 1978. Their only loss had been the narrow defeat against West Germany in February, a significant improvement on the previous year in which they had been beaten on three occasions. Their draw against the Republic of Ireland, however, acted as a stark reminder that qualification for the European Championship still hung in the balance.

The schedule of 1979 began on 7 February with a home qualifier against Northern Ireland. The Liverpool trio of Clemence, Phil Neal and Emlyn Hughes returned for the qualifier, a match that would prove to be one of the most impressive displays of force overseen by Greenwood. His team did take some time to make the breakthrough, which was not until the 25th minute, when Coppell delivered an inswinging cross into the box. Pat Jennings came off his line in vain, and Kevin Keegan scored yet another header for England. They grabbed their second a minute after the restart with Keegan turning provider for Bob Latchford, who claimed his fourth international goal with a downward header from the Hamburg man's floated delivery. Rattled by a goal so early in the half, Northern Ireland conceded again four minutes later, Watson getting on the end of a Brooking corner. Northern Ireland's slack marking at set pieces was again exposed in the 63rd minute when Brooking took another corner which this time found Keegan at the near post and he flicked on for

Latchford to complete a 4-0 rout. The win took England to the summit of their qualifying group, overtaking Northern Ireland in the process. It was England's biggest win since March 1977, and it had come against a side which had fielded players from the likes of Arsenal, Manchester United and Nottingham Forest.

Their rivalry resumed three months later for the British Home Championship in a rare occurrence of England playing the same opposition twice in a row. The match took place at Windsor Park in front of a crowd of 35,000. Hughes dropped out of the team for Phil Thompson, while Terry McDermott and Ray Wilkins came in for Brooking and Keegan. England began the game with great gusto and found themselves two up in the first 14 minutes. Watson scored the first and just three minutes later Coppell consolidated their lead. Another romp appeared on the cards for a short time, but the anticipated goal avalanche failed to materialise. Missing the presence of Keegan, England put in a mediocre performance as they began their defence of the Home Championship with a 2-0 win in a game best remembered for an altercation between Northern Ireland team-mates Gerry Armstrong and Terry Cochrane, involving the former kicking the latter up the backside in an off-the-ball incident.

England's second game of the Home Championship represented another landmark moment for black players. Having joined West Bromwich Albion from Orient in 1977 in a deal worth £110,000, Laurie Cunningham had quickly become one of the most exciting young players in the First Division. He made up a trio of West Brom players along with striker Cyrille Regis – who himself would go on to play for England – and midfielder Brendon Batson who were dubbed 'The Three Degrees' by manager Ron Atkinson, in a reference to the American vocal group. Though England at the time had a plethora of talented wide players, Cunningham forced his way into the reckoning. From a young age he had international ambitions, telling Brian Moore of ITV's *The Big Match* in an interview from 1975 how he wanted to become 'a great player if I can, not just a good one, not just an average one, to be a great one and to play for a country. Jamaica is supposed to have a good side coming up, because they're playing football over there now. If they're good in time and they ask me to play, I'd be glad to play. Or if it's England, I'll play for them as well.'

Cunningham would move to Real Madrid a month after his England debut, in the process becoming the first British player ever to turn out for the Spanish giants. In total, he would gather only six caps despite having a career in which he also played for Manchester United and Marseille. Tragically, Cunningham died in a car crash in 1989 aged 33 while contracted to Rayo Vallecano, leaving a legacy of being the first black player to play a competitive fixture for England.

Forward David Mills, the first £500,000 signing by a British club when he moved to West Brom from Middlesbrough in January 1979, had a short spell as Cunningham's team-mate at The Hawthorns. Mills said, 'He was a very talented player, very much an individual player. He was always a potential match-winner. In the England side in those days, they had wingers like Steve Coppell and Peter Barnes, so Laurie had a bit of competition. He was one of the so-called Three Degrees with Cyrille Regis and Brendon Batson at West Brom under Ron Atkinson. Laurie went to Real Madrid about six months after I joined West Brom. It possibly affected his chances with England, but I don't know.'

Kenny Sansom was the other player to make his debut against Wales, and there was a welcome return for Keegan to the side as well as a rare start for Joe Corrigan. Having guided Swansea City to promotion to the Second Division as player-manager, John Toshack led the line for the Welsh. The game would be a bore which ended 0-0. Though the result was far from pleasing for England, Wales were an in-form side having won four out of five games, their previous match being a 3-0 dismantling of Scotland with Toshack grabbing all three goals.

Scotland beat Northern Ireland in their second game of the Home Championship, leaving the competition finely poised. Scotland had started their own Euro 1980 qualifying campaign poorly with two losses from three games, so they hoped to rediscover some form in the encounter against their great rivals at Wembley on 26 May 1979. Greenwood performed a reshuffle following the draw with Wales, only Watson, Wilkins, Latchford and Keegan keeping their places. The game did not start well for England. Thompson failed to deal with a ball across the box which found the left foot of his Liverpool team-mate Kenny Dalglish, who instinctively teed up John Wark for a simple finish. The game was then held up when a fan wearing a tartan scarf made his way on to the field, the shaven-headed intruder embarrassing four policemen with his ducking and weaving before being belatedly caught, allowing play to resume. Even after the delay, Scotland remained in the ascendancy, and Clemence produced a wonderful one-handed save to spare Watson's blushes after the centre-back almost scored an own goal from an attempted clearance. On the stroke of half-time, however, England struck. Peter Barnes was just outside the D as he flicked the ball up after good work by Keegan, and then hit a low shot which crept through the defence to find the far corner of the net. Scottish shoulders did not drop following the setback, but after the hour mark their keeper George Wood spilled an angled shot by Wilkins with the ball falling kindly for Coppell to tap home. As fortuitous as this goal had been, England's third was brilliant. Starting the move in the centre circle, Keegan drove at the Scotland defence then played a quick one-two with Brooking before decisively slotting home for a 3-1 victory.

Wales played out a draw in the other match to confirm England as winners of the Home Championship for the second year running. Not since 1971 had England managed the feat of retaining the trophy. This would be the fifth last edition of the tournament, with the final Home Championship coming in 1984. The competition was not held in 1981 due to an escalation in the Troubles in Northern Ireland. Why a tournament that had taken place since before World War One was discontinued is open to debate. The falling attendances – one encounter between England and Wales at Wembley in 1983 attracted a mere 24,000 – were certainly among the reasons for its cancellation. Another was that the European Championship had grown dramatically over the previous 20 years, and the four nations had all become far more interested in qualifying for Europe's premier international competition, as well as, of course, the World Cup, than winning the Home Championship which had, by this stage, become little more than a sideshow. Putting aside whatever shortcomings it may have had, the Home Championship had delivered many exciting matches during its existence, and as such there have, on occasions, been calls to revive the competition.

England's following game was against Bulgaria in Sofia. Overwhelming favourites going into the clash, Greenwood's team did not disappoint. He had named an experienced side with the starting players each possessing caps totalling double figures. Keegan, once again wearing the captain's armband, opened the scoring in the 33rd minute with a well-placed finish. England's next goal came from a Brooking corner, Watson continuing his own impressive scoring run, and the final goal of the game was courtesy of a header from Peter Barnes. They had been fortunate to keep a clean sheet in the 3-0 win, as a quick free kick from the Bulgarians had at one point left the England defence ultimately requiring Keegan to clear off the line. In stiflingly hot conditions, however, Greenwood's men were a cut above their opponents, dictating the pace of the game by controlling possession and demonstrating clinical finishing. Now halfway through their group games, the result had placed England in a commanding position. The rest of the teams were all of similar quality and none had at this stage shown any sign of threatening England for top spot.

Following the Bulgaria match, the squad travelled to Stockholm to play Sweden in a friendly on 10 June. What would prove to be the biggest story of the game broke before kick-off. This was the first occasion that two black players started a match for the men's senior team with both Anderson and Cunningham making the team sheet. The game ended 0-0 thanks largely to Shilton, the keeper pulling off a string of good saves to keep the Swedes at bay. An early injury to McDermott had unsettled the side, and the Three Lions had created few clear-cut chances throughout, the most noteworthy falling to Hughes. Greenwood was surely content with how his side had performed in the calendar year up to this point. There had been no repeats of the substandard defensive displays which had occurred during the Denmark and Republic of Ireland games the previous year. In fact, England had only conceded once in their first six matches of 1979. June's international duty, however, was not over. The final game of their away triple-header was three days later in Vienna against Austria.

England were left stunned when they found themselves 2-0 down after half an hour, though a goal from Keegan – a header into an empty net – had given them a route back into the game. Hope faded once more when the Austrians restored their two-goal cushion as Kurt Welzl beat Shilton for the second time. A shell-shocked England made their way to the dressing room 3-1 down, fortunate that the deficit was not greater. For the only time in his tenure Greenwood substituted a goalkeeper, with Clemence brought on for Shilton. Another to make way was Latchford, Trevor Francis his replacement. This would be Latchford's final appearance in an England shirt, his international career ending with a respectable five goals from 12 appearances. The changes and Greenwood's team talk produced a response, and goals from Steve Coppell and Wilkins brought the scores level. Yet there was plenty of time for a final twist in the tale and Austria recovered superbly. Their perseverance was rewarded when goalscoring defender Bruno Pezzey bagged a brace to take the score to 4-3. Cunningham was thrown on in an attempt to turn the tide, but there was little he could do to prevent the loss. It had been over 15 years since England had last conceded four or more goals in a single game, and that had come against a Pelé-inspired Brazil in Rio de Janeiro. Austria were a good side and the previous year they had achieved one of their most famous results by beating West Germany in their final group match of the 1978 World Cup. A loss in itself would not have been too concerning for England, yet conceding four against Austria was alarming, especially as there were three key qualifiers to be played by the end of the year. Greenwood, therefore, was left with much to mull over as his players returned to their clubs.

The late 1970s had proven to be a pivotal period for black players. The resolve and endeavour displayed by those who suffered torrents of racial abuse from the stands would help to see an exponential growth in the number of black players across all levels of the game. Anderson's and Cunningham's places in history are secure, yet there are those who have undermined their legacies. Atkinson was one of the earliest managers to promote black players, notably in his first spell in charge of West Brom, spanning the late 1970s and early '80s. In later years, he emphasised what he had done to further the cause for greater inclusion by recalling that he once fielded nine black players in his Aston Villa side. 'Big Ron' spoke of his track record after being at the centre of a major storm in April 2004 when he infamously used a racial slur in reference to Chelsea defender Marcel Desailly. Atkinson was working as a pundit for ITV on coverage of the Monaco-Chelsea Champions League semi-final, first leg, and his ill-chosen words, intended to be off-air but picked up by microphones that ought to have been turned off, were broadcast in parts of the Middle East where the live feed continued. ITV later announced that Atkinson had resigned with immediate effect and he released a statement, in which he said, 'I made a stupid mistake which I regret. It left me no option but to resign.' Some still rushed to his defence. The most alarming attempt to justify the former Manchester United manager's comment came from TV presenter, and former Professional Footballers' Association chairman, Jimmy Hill, who said, 'It's the language of the football field – they do swear. In that context, you wouldn't think words like n***** were particularly insulting; it would be funny. Without wishing to insult any black men, it's us having fun. What about people who make jokes about my long chin?'

When England reached the final of the European Championship 17 years later – a feat that to date is only bettered by the World Cup triumph of 1966 – within seconds of the final kick of their 3-2 penalty shoot-out defeat to Italy, Marcus Rashford, Jadon Sancho and Bukayo Saka, who had all failed to convert their spot kicks, were subjected to vile messages across social media platforms. Discriminatory chants and outbursts on the terraces still occur, while the advent of social media has meant that players now receive abuse even when sitting in their homes. Viv Anderson's debut was without doubt a monumental moment in English football, yet over four decades later, the fight against racism rages on.

18

The Englishmen Abroad

OVER TIME, the globalisation of football has made it more common for England players to earn a living in foreign parts. At the European Championship of 1988, three of Bobby Robson's squad were playing on the continent – Gary Lineker at Barcelona and Glenn Hoddle and Mark Hateley with Monaco – whereas Alf Ramsey's World Cup winners of 1966 were all home-based.

Gerry Hitchens was the first player to earn a full cap for England while playing abroad after moving from Aston Villa to Inter Milan in 1961, and the forward scored in a friendly against Switzerland the following year. It would be 15 years before another achieved the same feat. Joe Baker was born in Liverpool but raised in Scotland and became something of a trailblazer in his days with Hibernian in 1959 as the first player to feature for England having never played for an English club. He scored on his debut in a 2-1 home win over Northern Ireland. Like Hitchens, Baker would go on to play in Italy where, at Torino in 1961, he linked up with Scotland's Denis Law, but England honours eluded him while he was overseas. Baker finally turned out in the Football League for Arsenal, Nottingham Forest and Sunderland, and it was with the Gunners that his England career was revived.

All-time great Jimmy Greaves was another who was not as fortunate as Hitchens when he, too, moved to Italy in 1961; despite having scored a hat-trick while with Chelsea in a 9-3 Wembley win against Scotland that year, Greaves was overlooked by England during his short spell with AC Milan. Not long after the striker had come home and joined Tottenham, Walter Winterbottom brought Greaves back into the international fold.

During the 1970s there was a shift in the perception of moving abroad with some of the biggest names in English football opting to leave the country, and one of these stars would contribute to this change more than any other. In 1977, Kevin Keegan had the world at his feet. Liverpool won the First Division in a tightly contested race with Manchester City as well as lifting the European Cup, and they came close to the treble, losing in the FA Cup Final to Manchester United. There were few clubs on the continent that could entice Keegan away from Anfield, but football in West Germany in the '70s was going through a renaissance and the Bundesliga had once more become one of the strongest leagues in Europe. It was Hamburg SV, a club that had just won the European Cup Winners' Cup, who would make a then-colossal offer to lure Keegan. Despite their European triumph, Hamburg had finished sixth in the Bundesliga and were looking for a marquee signing to help them challenge for the title.

Keegan's £500,000 move was, at the time, the highest fee paid for a British player and also a German transfer record. The price tag did not go down well initially with his team-mates. The 1977/78 season was neither a success for Hamburg nor Keegan with the club finishing in tenth place in the Bundesliga and the England star only registering six league goals. The low point of the season came at Anfield, of all places. Having drawn the first leg of the European

Super Cup 1-1, a tight game was expected, but Hamburg were hammered 6-0.

Branko Zebec, a Yugoslavian who had managed the likes of Bayern Munich and VfB Stuttgart, was brought in as head coach of Hamburg for the 1978/79 season, and his arrival signalled a change of fortune for Keegan's side. A great believer in the need for players to maintain a high level of fitness, Zebec was able to deliver the Bundesliga at his first attempt with Keegan excelling under his stewardship. Keegan would ultimately only spend three seasons with Hamburg (citing the strains that the high physical demands were taking as part of the reason behind his decision to leave), but his time in West Germany was undoubtedly a success. Playing abroad also hardly hampered his international career as he continued to play a key role for England throughout his spell in the German game.

Two other players to represent England while contracted to a foreign club in the 1970s were centre-back Dave Watson and forward Tony Woodcock. Like Keegan, they were lured to the Bundesliga, Watson moving from Manchester City to Werder Bremen in 1979. It was, however, an unhappy and brief association and he soon returned to England with Southampton. Having lifted the European Cup with Nottingham Forest that year, FC Cologne bought Woodcock for £600,000. Woodcock's time in West Germany was productive, and he narrowly missed out on a Bundesliga title medal in 1982 before his move to Arsenal.

Many England internationals during the era went abroad on loan in the close season, moves that were often financially beneficial to both the player and their parent club. In the Premier League era it is perhaps hard to imagine clubs risking their star players returning for pre-season injured or fatigued having played in another country all summer, but in the 1970s plenty of English teams were willing to take this gamble.

Trevor Francis, then of Birmingham City, moved to Detroit Express in 1978. By far among the best players in the North American Soccer League (NASL), Francis averaged over a goal a game in the United States, and he even returned to the club a year later – again on loan – after becoming the first British £1m player with Forest. Geoff Hurst also left the country for a fleeting loan spell during the same decade. The then-manager of South African side Cape Town City, former Ipswich Town and Crystal Palace goalkeeper Roy Bailey, was able to acquire the England legend for six games in 1973 while the forward was on the books of Stoke City. Three years later, another of England's 1966 team played in South Africa. Alan Ball turned out for Hellenic FC, a club also based in Cape Town, in 1976. Unusually, he became player-coach for American side Philadelphia Fury in 1978 despite only being on loan.

Ball made a permanent move to the NASL the following year, switching from Southampton to Vancouver Whitecaps. Thanks to an influx of money, North America became a popular destination. Having lost the sight in his right eye in 1972, Gordon Banks made a return to football following an invitation in 1976 from Fort Lauderdale Strikers, a newly formed team based in Miami. Banks flourished in the NASL. He was voted Goalkeeper of the Year and the Strikers won their division in his first season. As fate had it, he would also later play alongside his old bogey man George Best at the club. He was joined in the US by Bobby Moore when the World Cup-winning captain linked up with Seattle Sounders. Moore had already had a taste of the NASL during a loan spell at San Antonio Thunder in 1976, and he returned to the country after his contract with Fulham expired. Though he would only play seven league games for Sounders, landing Moore on a permanent deal was a coup for both the team and the NASL.

A good number of England internationals who headed to the United States were coming to the end of their careers, though there is one notable example of a player who moved in his prime. Dennis Tueart was in fine form for Manchester City during the 1977/78 First Division campaign when he left the club's fans stunned by moving to New York Cosmos. The winger was in his late 20s at the time and had only last played for England in the summer of 1977. There was a fair amount of pressure on Tueart; Cosmos had just lost Pelé to retirement and they had chosen the City man as a replacement for the legendary forward. Pelé, however, was not the only big-name player with the American side, and Tueart's team-mates included Franz Beckenbauer and Carlos Alberto.

In 1978, Tueart admitted in the *Daily Mirror* that he did have some regrets about his move to the States following the appointment of Ron Greenwood as England manager. He said, 'I liked Don Revie. He was good to me. But Don didn't like wingers. I couldn't see myself with an England future. Now under Greenwood, the pendulum seems to have swung the other way … America has given me financial security, but if Ron had got the job earlier it's possible I would have had second thoughts coming here.' Spending two years at the club, Tueart proved to be a steady supplier of goals for the Cosmos and won the NASL twice with them as well as the Soccer Bowl. Though his stint in America yielded plenty of medals, Tueart never played for England again following his move there, and he returned to Manchester City in 1979.

While many English players were enticed by the bright lights of the United States, there were those who made much more left-field moves abroad. Tottenham's Martin Chivers had been one of the most prolific forwards in the country during the early 1970s, but he began to find goals harder to come by, and in 1976 Swiss club Servette made a bid of around £80,000 for the striker. Servette had finished in second place in the Swiss Nationalliga A the season before and, hoping to win their first league title since the early '60s, they signed 'Big Chiv'. Though the England forward was unable to inspire a title success (this would come Servette's way the season after he left for Norwich City), Chivers was a big hit at the club and won both the Swiss Cup and the Swiss League Cup. Fellow England striker Malcolm Macdonald ended his playing days in Sweden, where he spent a brief spell with Djurgården in 1979.

Despite The Troubles in Northern Ireland, a handful of English players had spells in the Republic of Ireland during the 1970s. Banks made a single appearance for St Patrick's Athletic following a chance encounter at Heathrow Airport. The manager of the Irish club at the time, Barry Bridges (a former England international who had gained all his caps in 1965), had lost his first-choice keeper through injury when he happened to bump into his old team-mate. Banks offered to help him out, but Bridges was unsure about signing him at first and later recalled, 'Banksie said, jokingly, "What's wrong with me?" I said, "Banksie, you've only got one eye," and he said, "I can see the same balls with one eye that I could with two eyes, I'll come over and play for you."' Paid £500, an excellent appearance fee for the time, Banks rolled back the years and produced a series of saves to keep a clean sheet as St Patrick's beat Johnny Giles's Shamrock Rovers 1-0.

Geoff Hurst (Cork Celtic), Rodney Marsh (Cork Hibernians) and Bobby Charlton (Waterford) also played in the Republic of Ireland and each only figured in three league games for their clubs. Although many English players have played in the country over the years, very few England internationals have turned out for Irish clubs since the 1970s.

* * *

Interest would eventually wane in the NASL, and the league ultimately folded due to financial reasons. In 1996, Major League Soccer (MLS) was formed, and 11 years later saw the most famous transfer in the USA since Pelé had signed for Cosmos. David Beckham was only 31 when he moved to Los Angeles Galaxy in 2007, and he continued to feature for England despite playing outside Europe's top leagues. In time, other members of the 'Golden Generation', like Steven Gerrard, Frank Lampard, Ashley Cole and Wayne Rooney, would move to the United States.

On the European scene, unlike those such as Hitchens and Greaves, Keegan was able to not only feature consistently for England while playing on the continent, but also continue to thrive in an international shirt. In his time with Hamburg, 'Special K', as he was dubbed, won the Ballon d'Or twice – one of a select number of English players to be awarded the coveted prize. The other England internationals who ventured overseas at that time may not have enjoyed the same level of success, but they all played a part in proving that Englishmen could prosper abroad.

19

Waiting for a Call

THE HISTORY of English football is littered with accomplished players who never received the honour of representing their country at senior level. Bryan 'Pop' Robson – described by one-time West Ham United colleague Jimmy Greaves as 'the best striker England never capped' – Manchester United skipper Steve Bruce and Arsenal forward Kevin Campbell are just three who found that, for reasons best known to certain managers, the cap did not fit.

Considering the increase in substitutes permitted during matches, along with Don Revie's scattergun approach to calling up untested players, the 1970s should theoretically have been one of the easiest decades to win an England cap. Instead, scores of top-quality players failed to make the senior team, no matter how many trophies they had won in the domestic game. Of course, just because players missed out on a full cap it did not necessarily mean they were excluded from playing for their country.

* * *

Up until 1947 there were limited ways that the selectors could run the rule over players to assess whether they were candidates for an England call-up. Walter Winterbottom, regarded as England's first manager, devised the idea of introducing a reserve side that would play second-string teams of other European nations. The purpose, naturally, was to give players an opportunity to impress Winterbottom while also helping them to get a taste of international football. This side would become England's B team. Over the years, many successful players turned out at this level, but the advent of the England under-23 side in 1954 meant that the significance of the B team started to dwindle. All three of England's permanent managers in the '70s had played for the B team, yet not a single match took place during the tenures of Sir Alf Ramsey and Don Revie. Ron Greenwood, on the other hand, took a very different view of the side. In one of his first meetings with the FA International Committee, Greenwood stressed that he wanted to take a more continental approach to the youth teams and enlist some of the leading or most promising English managers to oversee each level to help him achieve his vision. Dave Sexton, Terry Venables, Howard Wilkinson and even Brian Clough were thus brought into the youth setup, and Bobby Robson was entrusted with the resurrected B team.

UEFA made a decision to revamp international youth fixtures in 1976 which led to a further limitation on who could play in the oldest grouping of the fledgling international teams, with the under-23s becoming the under-21s, although a small number of over-age players were permitted: goalkeeper Joe Corrigan had played more than 200 games for Manchester City and was pushing 30 years of age when he appeared at the European Under-21 Championship. Corrigan would become a favourite under Robson and set a record for the most appearances for the B team, with ten caps. Like Corrigan, many of the side received full caps, but there were those less fortunate. Gary Owen was Corrigan's team-mate and a teenager when he made his debut for City in 1975 and seemed destined to play for his country. A fee of around £500,000 was enough for Ron Atkinson's West Bromwich Albion to secure his services in 1979, and the midfielder became a regular for the West Midlands club. Owen played seven times for the B team in the late '70s and on 22 occasions for the under-21s, yet he never broke into the senior side. Future West Ham and Newcastle United manager Glenn Roeder made six B team appearances without winning a senior cap. Playing more than 100 games for both Queens Park Rangers and Newcastle, Roeder became one of the most cultured defenders of his era and perfected a step-over technique which became known as the 'Roeder Shuffle'.

Another who played for Newcastle and was surprisingly overlooked for senior international duty was Pop Robson. Born in Sunderland in 1945, 'Pop' (a nickname derived from the Rice Krispies advert featuring the characters Snap, Crackle and Pop and the pet names of Robson and two friends in childhood) began his professional career at the dreaded rivals of his boyhood club. The forward was an outstanding success at Newcastle, where he notched 97 goals in 244 appearances and was a member of the Inter-Cities Fairs Cup-winning side in 1969. His displays in a black and white shirt attracted the interest of West Ham manager Greenwood, who paid £120,000 to take him to Upton Park in February 1971. Robson had three seasons with the Hammers and the goals continued to flow: he was the top scorer in the First Division in the 1972/73 season with 28.

The following term, however, West Ham came dangerously close to being relegated and Robson, growing unsettled, transferred to Sunderland who at that point were in the second tier. Yet, after helping the Wearsiders to win promotion in 1976, Robson made a surprise return to West Ham. Over the next three years, he averaged almost a goal every other game, but even this impressive return was not enough to prevent West Ham from being relegated in 1978. He departed from the Hammers – having scored a total of 104 goals during his spells with the Londoners – for a second and final time the following year, and raised eyebrows again when he moved back to Sunderland. He would, once more, play a major role in a promotion-winning season for the Rokermen in 1980. Later he had spells at Carlisle United and Chelsea as well as a third stint with Sunderland. At the age of 38, he was still playing in the top flight and scored in his last game at that level in Sunderland's 2-0 win at Leicester in May 1984, a result that helped to safeguard their status in the old First Division. Robson never played for England, nor did he feature for the B team. The closest he came to the senior team was an appearance for the under-23s in the late 1960s.

So why did one of the most prolific scorers of the era not receive a full cap? The form of others was certainly a factor. At the start of the decade, Geoff Hurst, Martin Chivers and Allan Clarke were all reliable sources of goals for England, and Ramsey also had the likes of Peter Osgood at his disposal. Perhaps the player who was the biggest obstacle for English strikers hoping to break into the team was Southampton's versatile attacker Mick Channon, whose goals per appearance ratio is among the best of any England forward past or present. A possible perceived weakness in Robson's game may have been that he was not the tallest at 5ft 8in; however, he was able to make up for this by having a surprising leap, scoring with plenty of headers throughout his career. Even club bias (whether it exists or not) cannot apply in the case of Robson as he played for West Ham, a club that had produced a host of England internationals – and a manager for the national team who signed him. One consideration that unquestionably played a major role was the size of matchday squads at the time. In 1974, a year in which the country had three different managers, only four conventional strikers played for England.

In comparison, Fabio Capello in 2010 was able to field nine strikers (including debutants Bobby Zamora, Andy Carroll, Kevin Davies and Jay Bothroyd).

There were no England B team internationals for almost 21 years and when they returned with a match against West Germany in Augsburg in February 1978, Liverpool striker David Fairclough – dubbed 'Supersub' due to his happy knack of netting key goals when coming off the bench – scored the winner in a 2-1 victory, with club-mate Terry McDermott also on target. It came the day before Greenwood's senior outfit lost to West Germany by the same scoreline in Munich. Fairclough would never win a full cap and played only once for the under-21s. Of course, he suffered for having serious competition at club level from Kevin Keegan, John Toshack, Kenny Dalglish, David Johnson and, eventually, Ian Rush. There may have been no senior England caps for Fairclough, but there were two European Cup winners' medals with Liverpool: he was a substitute in 1977 and started in 1978.

Pop Robson and Fairclough were by no means on their own. Alan Ball was part of the engine room nicknamed 'The Holy Trinity' at Everton, though the other members of the trio would have differing fortunes in terms of the national team. Colin Harvey won a single cap, but Howard Kendall would play no higher than the under-23s. Kendall spent the majority of the '70s playing in the top tier for Everton, with whom he won the league in the 1969/70 season, and Birmingham City.

Another title-winning midfielder to finish his career uncapped was Jimmy Case. The Liverpool hard man, renowned for his tough tackling, was on the winning side in three European Cup finals and was named European Young Player of the Year. Case scored Liverpool's goal in their 2-1 loss to Manchester United in the 1977 FA Cup Final, but the man who netted the winner in that game was equally out of luck when it came to international football. Jimmy Greenhoff, who played alongside his brother, England international Brian, with the Red Devils after time at Leeds United, Birmingham and Stoke City, was not remarkably prolific in front of goal, but was one of the most admired strikers of his generation. Meanwhile, West Ham defender Billy Bonds (who was on one occasion an unused substitute for England), Aston Villa midfielder Dennis Mortimer, Sunderland goalkeeper Jim Montgomery and Chelsea legend Ron 'Chopper' Harris also played for the under-23s without ever reaching senior level for England.

Though the aforementioned were hugely unfortunate to miss out, a majority of those who did play for the under-23s in that era earned numerous caps. To name but a few, Channon, Keegan, Peter Shilton, Ray Clemence and Trevor Brooking all played for the youth team in the early 1970s. Ramsey took charge of the most England under-23 fixtures during his reign, and he treated the matches with the utmost seriousness: the harsh banning of Stoke's Alan Hudson, which was imposed because the midfielder once refused to play for the under-23s, was just one example of the manager's strictness. Revie, on the other hand, took a far more lenient attitude when Kevin Beattie failed to report for duty in 1974, continuing to select the defender and sparing him any punishment for his absence.

Unlike the senior side, England's development teams did qualify for tournaments during the '70s, though their fortunes were mixed. In 1976, an under-23 team containing Phil Thompson and Trevor Francis were resoundingly beaten 3-0 in the first leg of their European Championship quarter-final against Hungary in a freezing Budapest. Revie was there and, to compound a humbling experience, he and his players were pelted with snowballs as they left the field. Revie tried to remain positive afterwards but, though he maintained the result had flattered the hosts, he also acknowledged his side's shortcomings. He said, 'I was encouraged by the way the team knocked the ball about in their build-up. But I accept that is no good without any end product. The Hungarians deserved to win, but not by 3-0. If we can get a quick goal at Old Trafford, we are in with a chance.' England were able to avenge the loss in the return leg, where Case was among their scorers, but a 3-1 victory meant they were eliminated on aggregate. Two years later, a Tony Woodcock-inspired England beat Italy in the knockout stages of the inaugural European Under-21 Championship, Sexton's team meeting Yugoslavia in the semis. Vahid Halilhodžić (who would go on to manage Paris Saint-Germain and Japan, among others) scored a brace in the first leg, but a goal from Everton's Andy King gave England a chance going into the encounter at Maine Road. Halilhodžić, who had already been capped at senior level for Yugoslavia, scored his third goal in two games and although Leicester City defender Steve Sims grabbed an equaliser late on, it was not enough to take England to the final.

Out of all the England teams, it was the under-18s who enjoyed the most success. Winning the European Championship four times during the '70s, the side were coached by several managers over the course of the era including two former internationals in Gordon Milne and Tony Waiters. Clough's introduction in 1978, perhaps unsurprisingly, caused a stir. Ken Burton, a highly regarded youth coach but one who had not made it as a professional player, had been in charge of the team for more than three years when Clough was brought in to work alongside him. The two were unable to operate as joint managers, and their already strained relationship was damaged further when Clough's long-time ally Peter Taylor joined the setup. Burton decided that his position had become untenable and resigned shortly after they had won a tournament in Spain. It did not take long for Clough to follow him out of the door with former Crystal Palace midfielder John Cartwright installed as manager by the beginning of 1979. Clough's treatment of former Corby Town manager Burton had been entirely unprofessional. It is unclear what Clough wanted to achieve from his time as an England youth coach, but the way he treated others, the mediocre results to his name in the role and his decision to depart after only a short duration in charge cannot have put him in good stead with the FA when the England job came up once more in 1982.

Three of the midfielders who turned out for the England youth team would go on to amass more than 200 senior caps among them. Ray Wilkins was fast-tracked into the team, while Glenn Hoddle and Manchester United's Bryan Robson had to wait slightly longer to make their senior debuts for the Three Lions, first appearing at 22 and 23 respectively. Trevor Francis, Peter Barnes, Chris Woods and many more future internationals also represented the under-18s in the same era. The England youth team was struck with a tragedy in 1978. Peter Canavan, a highly rated apprentice at Ipswich Town, was killed in a car crash in which his club-mate David Geddis was injured. Canavan was only 17 years old.

Under the stewardship of Bobby Robson, the England B team achieved a near-flawless record. The only blip of sorts was a 1-1 draw against Malaysia during a tour of Asia and Oceania. Robson took a talented squad with him on the tour with future internationals Viv Anderson and Alan Kennedy included. They played New Zealand three times in June 1978, on each occasion beating them comfortably. Their biggest result of the tour, however, was an 8-0 thrashing of Singapore which remains to date the record victory for England's B team. Only two matches were played in 1979, and one of them, away to Austria B, was abandoned around the hour mark due to floodlight failure.

Greenwood's idea of bringing established English coaches into the national setup overall paid dividends. Robson, Venables and Wilkinson would all go on to manage England, though the latter, of course, only as a caretaker. Having been given an opportunity to impress the FA, Clough ultimately failed in his role. In the same decade that the man considered by many to be the greatest manager England never had was at the height of his powers, the country had also seen a whole host of talented, uncapped players light up English football. With squad sizes for international matches swelling at the turn of the millennium, it is entirely possible that fans will never again see a time when so many excellent players fail to gain the honour of being able to call themselves an England international.

20

Lions Roar Again

IN THE month that England played Denmark at Wembley, British football's transfer record was broken twice in a week as midfielder Steve Daley moved from Wolverhampton Wanderers to Manchester City for an exact fee of £1.4375m before Wolves used that money to buy striker Andy Gray from Aston Villa for £1.469m.

England manager Ron Greenwood, however, took the unusual step of naming a side without a conventional striker, with Kevin Keegan playing as the most central forward. Though he had witnessed his team concede four goals against Austria in their preceding game, Greenwood was not inclined to make wholesale changes, and the only players brought into the fold were Terry McDermott for Bob Latchford and Ray Clemence for Peter Shilton. By opting for a midfield trio consisting of McDermott, Ray Wilkins and Trevor Brooking, Greenwood chose an engine room with plenty of energy and physical presence as well as creativity.

The composition of Greenwood's squad had attracted criticism from some observers, and in his column in the *Liverpool Echo*, former Anfield favourite and one-cap England international Tommy Smith called on the manager to inject younger blood into his side. Smith said, 'I hope England struggle to beat Denmark … for Ron Greenwood's sake. The last thing I want Ron to do is trip over his loyalty to the players who have served him so far. That's why I would be happy to see England just scrape through by one or two goals – so Ron will have the perfect platform to experiment.' Smith added, 'Next time, I would like to see Ron bring some younger players into the squad.'

Despite Denmark being destined to finish bottom of the qualifying group, Smith's wish for a narrow England victory was granted, but that was no real surprise because the Danes had talent in their squad. Striker Allan Simonsen – who three years later would make a shock switch to Charlton Athletic – was playing for Barcelona at the time, and Frank Arnesen was integral in an Ajax team that had won the UEFA Cup earlier in the year. The fact that they had dispatched Northern Ireland 4-0 in the summer and scored three against England in their previous encounter was evidence enough that the Danes were not a team to be taken lightly.

After Denmark squandered an early opportunity, Keegan had an effort ruled out for offside. The disallowed goal was a warning for the Danes, one they did not heed. A cross from Phil Neal in the 17th minute somehow managed to evade several players before Keegan, who had drifted towards the far post, smashed the ball home with a half-volley. Clemence was required to make a smart stop in the second half, but England were the better team on the night and deserved their single-goal win. The result, though unspectacular, was a vitally important step towards qualification, and Greenwood said, 'Naturally, we are pleased to get two points, and it's nice to be in such a strong position in the group. We had an excellent first half. We played some great stuff and caused them a lot of problems. Then, they did exactly the same after the interval when we didn't close down as much as we might have done in midfield. We got a bit sloppy.' Denmark coach

Sepp Piontek pinpointed what he perceived as a weakness in the England side. He said, 'England look the best team in the group. But they still have some problems, particularly in midfield where there is a lack of variety. Only Keegan showed the ability to open our defence.'

England's next match was at Windsor Park on 17 October against Northern Ireland, who still had a chance of catching them. No fewer than three Arsenal players (Pat Jennings, Pat Rice and Sammy Nelson) and two from Manchester United (Jimmy Nicholl and Sammy McIlroy) lined up for Northern Ireland with Tottenham's Gerry Armstrong leading their attack. Greenwood, having chosen a midfield-heavy team against the Danes, unleashed both Trevor Francis and Tony Woodcock on the Irish. Greenwood's personnel changes would pay devastating dividends. Francis scored his first in the 18th minute with a low drive after collecting a through ball on the edge of the box. The pitch was sodden after heavy rain, and Woodcock's shirt was already caked in mud by the 33rd minute when he converted a cross by Francis. A goal from Northern Ireland's Vic Moreland early in the second half did nothing to dishearten England, and they were soon two goals to the good once more thanks to a rampant Francis. The fourth was scored by Woodcock and the game marked a significant moment in the forward's England career. His importance to the team would gradually grow over the years. Unlike many of his compatriots who played in the 1970s, Woodcock would represent his country at a World Cup, while he would also reach a tally of a more-than-respectable 16 goals from 42 caps.

With just over a quarter of an hour left, Neal received the ball in the Northern Ireland box and unselfishly attempted to tee up a team-mate. Slipping as he kicked the ball, the Liverpool defender made a hash of his pass; however, Nicholl, in his desperation to get to the ball first, diverted it into his own net. England employed differing tactics in the matches against the Danes and the Irish, adjustments that had paid off greatly, and individual performances in the two victories highlighted Greenwood's ability to get the best out of his players. The 5-1 win in Belfast left England on the cusp of qualification.

Greenwood's men knew before their next match that a win would guarantee them a place at the 1980 European Championship. Their opponents were Bulgaria, a side they had already comfortably beaten that year and one who had only won two qualifying games at that stage. As the England team were readying themselves on the night, there was an unexpected complication. A thick fog had set in around the stadium, and for the first time an international match at Wembley was postponed. The decision to rearrange the game for the following night had already been taken when the fog lifted before too long into the evening. The call-off had a significant knock-on effect. To make sure that he was not too fatigued for a league match that weekend, Hamburg recalled Keegan, and Greenwood took a diplomatic approach by choosing not to demand that he remained with his squad. Without their talisman, Norwich City's Kevin Reeves – one of two debutants – took Keegan's place. The other player making his first appearance for England was 22-year-old Glenn Hoddle. The Tottenham Hotspur midfielder would go on to become a key figure for the nation, featuring in both the 1982 and 1986 World Cups before then being appointed manager in 1996 and leading England on to the global stage in France two years later.

Regardless of the fact that the Bulgaria game had been put back 24 hours, Wembley was at near capacity. A corner early in the match gave Dave Watson two opportunities from close range, but his first shot was blocked and he skied his second. Watson, who had recently moved to Southampton after an ill-fated spell at West German side Werder Bremen, was presented with another chance soon afterwards. An unsophisticated corner-kick routine led to Hoddle receiving the ball just inside the box. The Bulgaria defence were far too slow in closing down the midfielder, and he was given enough time to chip the ball towards Watson. Hristo Hristov, the Bulgaria keeper, was too eager to come off his line, and Watson looped a header over him into an empty net. For the remainder of the half, England continued to dominate possession of the ball without carving out many more clear-cut chances. Hearts were in mouths soon after the restart when Clemence pulled off a brilliant one-handed save, the Liverpool keeper leaping to tip the ball over the bar. England refused to allow the scare to disrupt their rhythm and a cross from Wilkins was cleared only as far as Francis, who poked the ball in the direction of a lurking Hoddle. The gifted midfielder side-footed his shot with sublime finesse into the top corner to cap off a dream debut. There would be no late drama, no incredible comeback from the opposition. After all the tribulations of the era, Greenwood's team had made qualification look easy.

* * *

England had not successfully navigated a qualification campaign for a major tournament since Sir Alf Ramsey had taken them to the 1968 European Championship (they had qualified as World Cup hosts in 1966 and defending champions in 1970), until the victory against Bulgaria on 22 November 1979. Their first game of the 1980s was their final game of the group. The result – a 2-0 Wembley victory over the Republic of Ireland with a Keegan double – left England with a record of seven wins and a draw from eight games played. The 22 goals they had scored was at the time the most they had managed in a qualifying group; however, it should be noted that the five-team group was also the largest they had played in. What was perhaps most impressive about their record was that they had not played any minnows, such as Luxembourg.

In spite of the camaraderie and undoubted talent in the squad, Euro 1980, held in Italy as the final stages of the competition had been in 1968, represented a poor return to tournament football for England. There was, however, little genuine optimism back home, which was in part down to the fact that star player Keegan had only just recovered from a knee injury in time for the competition. Their group was also far from easy: Belgium, Italy and Spain. 'People talk as if Italy and England are the only teams in our group,' Guy Thys, Belgium's manager, said before the opening fixture. 'Of course, I am concerned with them, but they worry me far less than West Germany or Holland would.' Thys was right not to fear England. After drawing their opener against Belgium 1-1, Wilkins scoring, the Three Lions stayed in Turin and lost 1-0 to Italy before restoring some pride by beating Spain 2-1 in Naples where Brooking and Woodcock both struck. While England crashed out at the group stage, Belgium would go on to reach the final where they would lose to West Germany. England's tournament would ultimately be best remembered not for events on the pitch, but for those on the terraces. Hooliganism had already become a much-talked-about blight in English football during the 1970s, but the severity of the violence at Euro 1980 caused a major shift in the discourse.

England then made a mediocre start to the qualification campaign for the 1982 World Cup, but a thumping 3-1 win over Hungary in Budapest – Brooking scoring twice and Keegan converting a penalty – was the boost they badly needed. Greenwood, however, stunned his players on the flight home by informing them he had already made his mind up that he would be resigning as manager. The squad pleaded with him to reconsider and, encouraged by their backing and the victory, Greenwood agreed to remain in post. England, though, were still not out of the woods. Before the trip to Hungary, they had lost 2-1 to Switzerland in Basel, where the hooligan element among the travelling support brought more shame on the nation. And three months after England appeared to have found their way in Hungary, there was further embarrassment with another 2-1 defeat, this time to Norway on an infamous night in Oslo. A 1-0 win over Hungary at Wembley through Paul Mariner's goal then sealed the deal. Though they had to settle for being runners-up in the group behind the Hungarians, England had reached their first World Cup in 12 years.

They eased through the first round of the tournament in Bilbao with a 100 per cent record, Bryan Robson scoring twice – the first goal after only 27 seconds – and Mariner also netting in a 3-1 opening win against France. Francis and Mariner secured a 2-0 win over Czechoslovakia and the former scored the only goal against Kuwait.

But England found themselves in a tricky second-stage group that included West Germany and Spain and, having been denied the services of Keegan and Brooking due to injury until the final match against the hosts when the pair came off the bench (Keegan missing a glorious chance), they drew both games 0-0. Despite being unbeaten, England were out.

Liverpool midfielder McDermott had featured in every qualifier and made the squad that Greenwood took to Spain, but surprisingly played no part in the tournament. Recalling qualification, McDermott said, 'We were getting beaten 2-0 in Switzerland and they brought me on. I scored about ten minutes into the second half. Once we got back to 2-1, you expected to get an equaliser and maybe go on and win the game – but we lost. Then we lost in Norway and the

Norwegian commentator [Bjørge Lillelien] was shouting "Maggie Thatcher, can you hear me? Maggie Thatcher … your boys took a hell of a beating"! It was an up-and-down campaign. We also lost in Romania and drew 0-0 with them at Wembley, but the significant thing was winning in Hungary between the defeats in Switzerland and Norway.' McDermott added, 'If you go back to when I played for England, we didn't qualify for the World Cup in 1978, and '82 was disappointing. We were lucky to get to Spain and we were unbeaten there, but didn't get beyond the second phase.'

Greenwood, though, had seen the job through and after England returned home, he finally decided to take his leave. He died on 9 February 2006, aged 84.

Epilogue

Pain and Redemption

FOR ALL their failings, fickle fate was one of England's toughest opponents in what proved to be the most depressing decade in the history of the national team. The loss of their status as World Cup holders, subsequent absence from major tournaments (until appearing at the 1980 European Championship finals) and the manner in which England were thwarted gave the impression that the country who gave birth to football were being punished for hubris.

Indeed, nemesis began to take its toll with the cruellest blow of all at the 1970 World Cup in the heat of Mexico where England's hopes of defending their title evaporated against the nation who had suffered at their hands in the final four years earlier. West Germany, however, never looked like they were destined to exact such devastating retribution. After all, England led 2-0 in their quarter-final and Sir Alf Ramsey's side were in complete command before their colossal collapse. Much of the blame for the 3-2 defeat, some of it unfairly, was levelled at stand-in goalkeeper Peter Bonetti. Most believe that had Gordon Banks not been ruled out with a stomach upset, England would have won. Yet, as a counterpoint to the hard-luck story, the withdrawal by Ramsey of Bobby Charlton – albeit understandable in some respects as the Manchester

United star, then 32, tired in the punishingly hot conditions – was seen by many as a pivotal moment.

Under three and a half years later, the hands of another keeper, Poland's Jan Tomaszewski, signalled the beginning of the end for Ramsey. Tomaszewski produced a performance of defiance, eccentricity, occasional brilliance but, above all, extraordinary good fortune to deny England a place at West Germany's table for the 1974 World Cup. By the end of that tournament, having also barred England's route to the European Championship finals of 1972 and won that title by beating the Soviet Union, the Germans were again world champions themselves.

Ramsey, who had gradually broken up the ageing nucleus of his 1966 World Cup-winning side, was gone himself before West Germany emulated England with their triumph on home soil. Given all he had achieved, being sacked was a cruel indignity to inflict on such a loyal servant to the English game. Bobby Charlton said, 'Alf Ramsey gave all of us in English football our greatest moment ... he was professional to his fingertips and as popular with the players as any manager I've seen. He was a winner and without him, England would not have won the World Cup.' Before Ramsey's departure, the likes of Charlton, captain Bobby Moore, World Cup Final hat-trick hero Geoff Hurst, the brilliant Banks and all but two – Alan Ball and Martin Peters – of their immortal team-mates had been consigned to England's history. Ramsey blooded future stars like Peter Shilton and his great goalkeeping rival, Ray Clemence, plus Kevin Keegan and Trevor Brooking.

After Joe Mercer's short spell as caretaker manager, Don Revie introduced many more new faces during his disastrous stint in charge, but England were once again missing from the party when Czechoslovakia ended West Germany's reign as European champions in 1976. Managing England, Revie found, was a very different proposition to leading his famous Leeds United side. The promise of World Cup qualification was already slipping away in the summer of 1977 when Revie did so himself. Money always talked where Revie was concerned and he struck gold in the oil-rich United Arab Emirates. Turning his back on his country in such a way made him the Aunt Sally of English football and his critics were quick to queue up and take aim like those on a fairground.

A trusted figure was required to restore England's tarnished reputation. Enter former West Ham boss Ron Greenwood, a manager with a similar pedigree to the previous incumbent. Like Revie, Greenwood had only managed one club before becoming England manager; both men had also created footballing institutions at their respective clubs; both had guided their sides to FA Cup Final glory and European silverware; both were among the great tacticians of their era. When it came to management styles, however, they differed. In his time in the England hot seat, Revie made a habit of upsetting players, but Greenwood was generally a lot more approachable throughout his managerial career. There were also rarely surprises in Greenwood's England squad announcements and he was able to strike a good balance between youth and experience in his team selections.

That owed much to the number of players called up: Greenwood was far less prone to making sweeping changes to his side, while Revie threw caps around like confetti. Yet that in itself was a strange change of tack for Revie, who in his Leeds days revelled in regularly naming the same side and working closely with a tightly knit group of players.

Greenwood's tenure, of course, was not without errors. The decision to name a youthful and experimental attack against Luxembourg in 1977 (a game that England only won 2-0) was surely a mistake in a match they needed to win comprehensively to maintain realistic hope of World Cup qualification. In his defence, however, this was a game that was very early in his reign, and two specific results under Revie – the narrow victory over Finland and the loss against Italy – had already made qualifying a formidable task.

In common with all England managers towards the end of a period in office, Greenwood came in for plenty of criticism. For instance, there were many who believed he was far too defensively minded during the 1982 World Cup; the fact that England only managed six goals from their five matches in Spain would suggest that the criticism was far from baseless. As he failed to take an England team to the semi-finals of a major competition, Greenwood might not rank alongside the likes of Ramsey, Sir Bobby Robson and Gareth Southgate, but a win percentage of 60 and a qualification record of two out of three tournaments – they also reached the European Championship in 1980 – places him above the majority who have held the top job in English football. Credit, ultimately, has to go to Greenwood for bringing the Lions back from the wilderness.

Bibliography

Books:

Anderson, J., *Sky Sports Football Yearbook, 2016/17* (Headline Publishing, 2016)

Bell, C., Cheeseman, I., *Colin Bell: Reluctant Hero* (Mainstream Publishing, 2014)

Betts, G., *England Player Records* (G2 Entertainment, 2019)

Brown, J., Ross, P., *England: The Complete Record* (deCoubertin Books, 2018)

Gibbs, N., *England – The Football Facts* (Facer Books, 1988)

Glasper, H., *Middlesbrough: A Complete Record* (The Breedon Books Publishing Company, 1993)

Greenwood, R., *Yours Sincerely* (Willow Books, 1984)

Hughes, E., *Crazy Horse* (Arthur Barker Limited, 1980)

Keegan, K., *My Life in Football* (Macmillan, 2018)

Powell, J., *Bobby Moore: The Life and Times of a Sporting Hero* (Robson Books, 1993)

Shaw, P., *The Book of Football Quotations* (Ebury Press, 2008)

Sutcliffe, R., *Revie: Revered and Reviled* (Great Northern, 2010)

Vernon, L., Rollin, J., *Rothmans Football Yearbook 1976/77* (Queen Anne Press, 1976)

Television:

BBC Sport

ITV Sport

Sky Sports News

Yorkshire Television

Magazines and periodicals:
Free Lions – Football Supporters' Association fanzine
Daily Mail
Daily Mirror
Daily Star
Daily Star Sunday
Daily Telegraph
Sunday Telegraph
Sunday People
The Times
Birmingham Daily Post
Birmingham Evening Mail
Liverpool Daily Post
Liverpool Echo
London Evening Standard
Newcastle Evening Chronicle
Reading Evening Post
Western Daily Press

Online sources:
bbc.co.uk
dailymail.co.uk
englandfootballonline.com
englandstats.com
fourfourtwo.com
independent.co.uk
irishtimes.com
itv.com
nytimes.com
stokesentinel.co.uk
theguardian.com
11v11.com